# WISECRACKS

Other humorous quotation books by Prion

Des MacHale
Wit
Wit Hits The Spot
Wit On Target
Wit- The Last Laugh
Wit Rides Again

Aubrey Dillon Malone
The Cynics Dictionary

Stephen Robins
The Importance of Being Idle
How to be a Complete Dandy

Michelle Lovric
Women's Wicked Wit

Rosemarie Jarski
Hollywood Wit - Classic Off-Screen Quips and Quotes

# WISECRACKS

## Rosemarie Jarski

PRION

First published in Great Britain in 1998
This paperback edition published in 2000 by

Prion
an imprint of the
Carlton Publishing Group
20 Mortimer Street
London W1T 3JW

10 9 8 7 6 5 4 3

A catalogue record of this book is available from the
British Library

ISBN 1-85375-357-2

All pictures courtesy of The Vintage Magazine Co.

Printed in Great Britain
by Mackays

# CONTENTS

# INTRODUCTION

> **A wisecrack is something we think of 24 hours too late.**
>
> *George Burns*

Hollywood didn't invent the wisecrack. As the linchpin of American verbal humor, it was making 'em laugh when Tinseltown was still just a twinkle in the eye of Cecil B. DeMille. Wisecracking has always been the first language in New York – wisecrack-capital of the world. In Jewish culture, there is a long tradition of wisecracking in the face of adversity. In literary circles, Mark Twain's pioneering wisecracking dialogue paved the way for Ring Lardner, Damon Runyon and the legendary wisecrackers of the Algonquin Set. In mob culture and detective pulp fiction, the wisecrack is every wise-guy's verbal equivalent of his gun. In vaudeville it was the stock-in-trade of every comedian. From this wealth of wisecracking humor Hollywood begged, borrowed, and just plain stole to groom the wisecrack for movie stardom.

The wisecrack's rise to fame on the silver screen was limited by the silent nature of the medium in the early days. For nearly three decades, it was trapped in the clumsy shape of the comic title card – usually as an egregious pun. Its big break came in 1927 with the coming of sound. Overnight, 'pictures' turned into 'talkies', sightgags turned into wordgags, and the wisecrack turned into a star.

And it has remained a star to this day. Changing tastes in humor over the years have done nothing to dull its comic sparkle. The wisecrack is as much a staple of Hollywood movies as the kiss, the car-chase and the happy ending.

The timeless appeal of the wisecrack is not hard to figure out. A smart quip, a pithy putdown, a snappy comeback – whatever shape it takes, it is the perfect humorous soundbite. That humor is, at its best, sharp and sardonic, perfectly tuned for exposing hypocrisy and dissing authority. 'When we see a pompous fellow in a high silk hat swelled up with his own importance and sniffing and sneering at folks as they pass,' said Groucho Marx, 'we do exactly what the rest of the world would like to do. We heave a ripe tomato at his hat.' A ripe tomato, that's a wisecrack.

In the movies, of course, there is the added thrill of seeing the ripe tomato pitched by a favorite Hollywood idol with the kind of pin-point precision and split-second timing we can only dream about in real life. (Hesitation of any kind is instant death to a wisecrack, no matter how brilliant.)

Despite its popularity, there are some – mostly in elitist critical circles – who dismiss the wisecrack as second-rate comedy, a cheap shot at humor, at best, a kind of bargain-basement wit. Wit is held up as highbrow, profound, polished: wisecracks are looked down on as lowbrow, hollow and disposable.

The wisecrack has no pretensions to profundity or posterity, it's true. But that does not mean there's *never* any wisdom in a wisecrack. In screwball and *film noir*, it can be multi-layered and charged with meaning. That said – and as anyone who has ever seen an Abbott and Costello movie knows – it can also be pretty dumb. More pro-fun than profound. Low on thinks but high on laughs. Never underestimate the value of a laugh, however simple. As critic Pauline Kael said, 'Shallow entertainment helps keep us sane'.

This collection welcomes wisecracks of all IQs – from the smart through the silly to the treasurably bad. Making 'em laugh is what counted in their selection irrespective of which actors spoke them or what films they're from. They run the gamut of pictures from A to B, and encompass all genres from frothy musicals to hard-boiled *noir*, run-of-DeMille epics to Looney Tunes cartoons.

Some of the richest pickings come from 'screwball' pictures, those larky romantic comedies that first delight-ed audiences in the 30s and 40s. Screwball dialogue is constructed as a comic duel fought with the points of wisecracks, and none fenced funnier or faster than Rosalind Russell and Cary Grant in the fabulous *His Girl Friday*.

'He treats me like a woman.'

'How did I treat you? Like a water-buffalo?'

'He's kind and he's sweet and he's considerate. He wants a home and children.'

'He sounds more like a guy I ought to marry.'

Their battle of words is also a battle of wills, and a battle of the sexes. At another level, still, it is a courtship dance, choreographed in wisecracks. We get a kick out of watching the stars spar with each other, secure in the knowledge that differences will be resolved, obstacles will be overcome, and they will be in each other's arms by the time the credits roll.

The externalization of sexual desire and conflict through wisecracking dialogue is a strategy also used in *film noir*. In both genres, it was the screenwriters' ingenious way of circumventing the prissy film censorship laws of the period which effectively banned any overt reference to sex. What could not be said directly could be wrapped up discreetly in a wisecrack – 'a harmless little joke' – and slipped past the Hays Office. Not that they were entirely fooled. As one frustrated censor put it, 'We know what they're saying, we just can't prove that they're saying it.'

Paradoxically, it is the eschewal of explicit sexual reference that makes screwball and *film noir* so sexy. When censorship laws loosened up in 1968, sex was made graphic both visually and verbally. Writers were no longer required to invent artful wisecracking routines to elude the censor's radar, and we were no longer required to use our imaginations because everything was spelt out for us: subtext had become text. About this time a lot of the fun went out of watching movies.

The cracks in this collection come mostly from movies made when the old studio system reigned supreme. The moguls who ran the studios had no time for well-bred witticisms that might coax an inward smile. What they wanted were big laughs because big laughs = big audiences = big revenues. They drafted in streetwise scribes like Billy Wilder and Ben Hecht (both ex-newspapermen) whose scabrous knack with a crack delivered big laughs aplenty. Wilder's *Ball of Fire* and Hecht's *Nothing Sacred* typify the slangy, tangy idiom of movies in the 30s and 40s. It was a time when talkies were at their talkiest, wisecracks were at their most cracking, and entertainment was at its most entertaining; a golden age that shows no sign of tarnishing.

In its heyday, the Dream Factory had so many throw-away lines to throw away that supporting players often caught a piece of the verbal action. One of the best of these 'know-the-face-not-the-name' actors was Clifton Webb. He was Hollywood's answer to Noël Coward, and the original Mr Belvedere. With his waspish wisecracks in the stylish *film noir*, *Laura*, he not only stole the scene but the picture. Monty 'The Beard' Woolley did the same in the deliciously acerbic comedy, *The Man Who Came to Dinner*.

Female supporting characters were often cast in the role of wisecracking domestic (Thelma Ritter, Marjorie Main); wisecracking tart with a heart (Joan Blondell, Jan Sterling); or wisecracking best friend of the leading lady (Eve Arden, Una Merkel) – she was the girl who who always got the laughs but never got the leading man. (Not such a bum rap if it was a Jerry Lewis movie.)

Of the star names, the oldest and one of the greatest, is W.C. Fields. (His initials stand for Wise Crack – what else?) Kenneth Tynan said he looked and sounded like a cement-mixer. Fields had all the credentials of a wise-cracker: a love of the booze, a hatred of the world, and a big mouth. He famously once said that he gave to only one charity – the F.E.B.F. (Fuck Everybody But Fields). A sworn enemy of all things sentimental and nice, especially kids, moms and wives, in today's climate of political correctness, the wisecracks of W.C. Fields are a breath of fresh air.

'Why is life worth living?' That's the question posed by Woody Allen – the best wisecracker of contemporary cinema--in his movie, *Manhattan*. Top of his list of reasons is one name: Groucho Marx. For dazzling invention and verbal bravado, the wisecracks of Groucho Marx are unsurpassed. Zany *non sequiturs*, outrageous puns and quicksilver quips snap, crackle and pop out of his moustachioed mouth like a comic version of Tourette's Syndrome. His twin passions were money and women (strictly in that order), and when they spontaneously combust in a wisecrack the result is an explosion of laughter that refreshes the parts conventional wit could never reach. 'Have the florist send some roses to Mrs Upjohn and write "Emily, I love you" on the back of the bill' more than makes up for his brother's harp solos. Woody was right.

As the quintessential screwball hero in his early career, Cary Grant's wisecracking style was almost as fast and frenetic as Groucho's. It mellowed into an easygoing elegance. Cary Grant's wisecracks disarm with charm. He could tell you to go to hell in such a way that you'd actually look forward to the trip.

Cary Grant mastered the wisecrack as a weapon of seduction. Humphrey Bogart mastered it as a weapon of humiliation. 'Respect' was the name of the game on the mean streets he went down in movies like *The Big Sleep*. In any powerplay, wordplay mattered as much as gunplay. Under threat, Bogey could shoot from the hip, but when he wanted to go for the kill, he always shot from the lip.

A comic spin on the cynical wiseguy wisecrack set

Bob Hope on the road to stardom. Hope's schtick was the tough guy who turned yeller with the wind. He tried to cover up his fear with wisecracks. His unstoppable flow of cocky-cum-cowardly cracks brought comic relief to movie audiences during the dark days of the Second World War and made him an entertainment institution. To this day, his name is synonymous with 'wisecrack'.

Bob Hope's name is also forever linked with Bing Crosby. They were one of many movie double acts whose jokey banter made an ideal home for the wisecrack. Comic duo Laurel and Hardy are best known for their visual gags but their verbal gags could be equally funny. Stan's solecisms, being unwitting, may not be wisecracks in the strictest sense, but their logical illogicality has the same effect of stunning the listener into submission, and only a pedant would deny us the pleasure of them here.

The greatest romantic comedy team was William Powell and Myrna Loy. Powell and Loy are the Astaire and Rogers of wisecracking. First paired in *The Thin Man*, they quip-stepped their way deftly and amusingly together through 13 more pictures in a partnership lasting 14 years – 'longer than any of my marriages' Myrna Loy wryly observed.

Myra Loy is part of a long and illustrious line of

female wisecrackers of the classic Hollywood era. Rosalind Russell, Jean Arthur, Ginger Rogers, Jean Harlow, Joan Crawford, Carole Lombard, Barbara Stanwyck, Katharine Hepburn, Irene Dunne, Lucille Ball... the roll of honor is an endless list of legends that matches – surpasses – the roll-call of male wisecrackers and could not begin to be emulated today. These women were not only funny. They were smart and tough-talking and uninhibited and sexy and what's more, women's lib hadn't even been invented.

Jean Harlow combined toughness with drop-dead glamour. She was the original 'platinum blonde' whose bee-sting pucker packed as powerful a punchline as it did a kiss. Clark Gable got a taste of both when he co-starred with her in racy little flicks like *China Seas* and *Red Dust*, before her sadly premature death at the age of only 26.

Barbara Stanwyck was one of Hollywood's most versatile wisecrackers, male or female. As the feisty heroine in comedies like *The Lady Eve*, or *femme fatale* in thrillers like *Double Indemnity*, she was always poised to parry an impertinent come-on with a sparky comeback.

The most potent concentration of female comedic power was distilled into one film of 1939. *The Women* is a paean to wisecracking bitchiness. It was co-scripted by Anita Loos, Jane Murfin and an uncredited F. Scott

Fitzgerald. (Have fun guessing which quips might be from his quill.) A 135-strong, women-only cast headed up by Joan Crawford and Rosalind Russell let rip with ripostes sharper than their fingernails and caustic enough to strip the 'jungle-red' varnish right off. *The Women* is a masterpiece of sustained high-octane wisecracking and a masterclass for any aspiring quipster.

One woman who never needed any lessons in the art was that singular sensation known as Mae West. She was a born quiptomaniac. She never made a film till she was 40, but she one-lined her way into myth with her unique brand of risqué repartee. Mae West put the sex into humor and the humor into sex. Her shameless enjoyment of the men in her life – and the life in her men – thrilled audiences, saved the fortunes of Paramount, but outraged the moral majority. The Film Censorship Code of 1934 was brought in mainly to crack down on her wisecracks. It finally killed her film career, but she lives on through her wisecracks, many of which have become part of our everyday language as assuredly as anything from Shakespeare.

Mae West, Groucho Marx, Cary Grant and Bob Hope were among the comic talent who honed their wise-cracking skills in vaudeville before transferring them to movies on their transition to sound. In talkies, words mattered, therefore voices mattered. The human voice

replaced in part the physical comedy of pure pan-
tomimists like Buster Keaton and Charlie Chaplin (who
fiercely resisted talkies). All the great comic stars of the
early talkies had distinctive voices – 'personality voices'
as they were known in the trade. They were an integral
part of their comic characterizations. In reading their
words, each individual voice seems to resonate off the
cold page as warmly familiar and instantly recognizable
as the voice of our best friend.

So closely do we identify voice and dialogue, it's easy
to forget that most actors did not make it up themselves.
Mae West and W.C. Fields were two of those rare comics
who *were* clever enough to invent most of their own
wisecracks. The majority depended on writers. The
Marx Brothers were blessed with geniuses like Morrie
Ryskind, George S. Kaufman and S.J. Perelman.
(Perelman described working for them as being 'no
worse than playing piano in a house of call'.) Bob Hope
hired his own private gaggle of gagmen to ensure his
'mots' were 'bons.' And where would Bogey's cool deadpan delivery have been without the cool deadpan humor
of Raymond Chandler to deliver? Writing comedy is no
joke. So much sweated blood goes into its creation, you
wonder whether the right names get to be in lights.

They don't write 'em like they used. All the more
reason, then, to relish a time when they did. Get the low-

down on who said what to whom, when, and where. Make believe you're Groucho or Mae and roadtest the lines in the privacy of your own living-room. (As we learn to kiss by imitating our favorite movie stars, so we learn to wisecrack.) Or just settle back and reach for the popcorn because, as someone once quipped, you ain't heard nothin' yet.

Rosemarie Jarski, 1998

# COMMUNICATION

# NAMES

— Oh, Monsieur Kornblow!
— Call me Montgomery.
— Is that your name?
— No, I'm just breaking it in for a friend.

> Lisette Verea and Groucho Marx
> **A Night in Casablanca** 1946

I am Giacomo, a lover of beauty and a beauty of a lover.

> Danny Kaye
> **The Court Jester** 1956

— My name's Mike.
— A pretty masculine handle for such a feminine pile of goods.

> Jane Russell and Bob Hope
> **Son of Paleface** 1952

My name is Grace, but everyone calls me Gracie for short.

> Gracie Allen
> **Six of a Kind** 1934

2

You may call me Streetcar because of my desire for you.

> Pepe Le Pew
> **A Scent of the Matterhorn** 1961

It took more than one man to change my name to Shanghai Lily.

> Marlene Dietrich
> **Shanghai Express** 1932

Johnny's such a hard name to remember and so easy to forget.

> Rita Hayworth to Glenn Ford
> **Gilda** 1946

The girls call me Pilgrim because every time I dance with one, I make a little progress.

> Bob Hope
> **The Ghost Breakers** 1940

I call everyone Babe.

> Clark Gable
> **Idiot's Delight** 1939

You're a disgrace to our family name of
Wagstaff, if such a thing is possible.

> Groucho Marx
> **Horse Feathers** 1932

Do you suppose I could buy back my
introduction to you?

> Groucho Marx to Chico Marx
> **Horse Feathers** 1932

— Do you know who I am?
— No. Isn't there anyone around here who
can tell you?

> George Barbier and Alison Skipworth
> **Tillie and Gus** 1933

— Call me a cab.
— Okay, you're a cab.

> Gene Kelly and Donald O'Connor
> **Singin' in the Rain** 1952

# GENERAL TALK

— Hello, Charlie. I didn't know we were still
speaking.
— Sure we're speaking, Jedediah. You're fired.

Joseph Cotten and Orson Welles
**Citizen Kane** 1941

Elaine communicates with my brother and
myself almost entirely by rumor.

Jason Robards
**A Thousand Clowns** 1965

If you want news to travel fast, telephone,
telegraph or tell a woman.

Eve Arden
**Women in the Wind** 1939

In my mind, you are buried in cement right
up to the neck. No, up to the nose, it's much
quieter.

Richard Burton to Elizabeth Taylor
**Who's Afraid of Virginia Woolf?** 1966

If I'd known how much you talked, I'd never have come out of my coma.

Charles Laughton
**Witness for the Prosecution** 1957

You talka too much. From now on you keepa your hands shut.

Chico Marx to Harpo Marx
**Go West** 1940

'Shut up?' You can't talk to me like that until after we're married.

Bob Hope to Jane Russell
**Son of Paleface** 1952

# TOUGH TALK

I got him right where he wants me.

Sylvester the Cat
**Hippety Hopper** 1949

— I am Speedy Gonzales, the fastest mouse in Mehico.

— We're not in Mexico now, mouse.

Speedy Gonzales and Daffy Duck
**Music Mice-Tro** 1967


The next person says Merry Christmas to me, I'll kill him.

Myrna Loy
**The Thin Man** 1934


Well, what shall we hang, the holly or each other?

Peter O'Toole to Katharine Hepburn
**The Lion in Winter** 1968


— You almost scared me to death.

— Almost doesn't count.

Ruth Gordon and George Segal
**Where's Poppa?** 1970

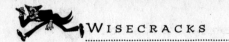

Well, well...the people you run into when
you're not carrying a gun.

Ida Lupino
**The Man I Love** 1947

He says he'd like to do her nails right down
to the wrist with a big buzz saw.

Joan Fontaine
**The Women** 1939

— If you touch me, I'll call a cop.
— If I touch you, you'll call an ambulance.

Jack Mower and Humphrey Bogart
**They Drive by Night** 1940

A better dame than you called me a liar and
they had to sew her up in 12 different places.

Mae West
**I'm No Angel** 1933

– What are you rebelling against?
– What've ya got?

> Mary Murphy and Marlon Brando
> **The Wild One** 1953

– Remember, this gun is pointed right at
your heart.
– That is my least vulnerable spot.

> Humphrey Bogart and Claude Rains
> **Casablanca** 1942

– Let's you and me have a heart-to-heart talk.
– What would *you* use?

> Bernard Nedell and Eve Arden
> **Slightly Honorable** 1940

I've met a lot of hard-boiled eggs in my life,
but you – you're 20 minutes.

> Jan Sterling to Kirk Douglas
> **Ace in the Hole** 1951

He has a heart of gold – only harder.

> Adolphe Menjou about Lionel Stander
> **A Star is Born** 1954

Compared to him an elephant's skin is tissue paper.

> Joan Crawford about Clark Gable
> **Dancing Lady** 1933

Given a choice of weapons with you, sir, I should choose grammar.

> Halliwell Hobbes
> **Lady for a Day** 1933

Shall I spit in Crystal's eye for you? You're passing up a swell chance, honey. Where I spit, no grass grows ever.

> Paulette Goddard to Norma Shearer
> **The Women** 1939

I am sitting here, Mr Cook, toying with the idea of removing your heart and stuffing it like an olive.

> Walter Connolly to Fredric March
> **Nothing Sacred** 1937

My father made him an offer he couldn't refuse. Luca Brasi held a gun to his head, and my father assured him that either his brains or his signature would be on the contract.

> Gianni Russo
> **The Godfather** 1972

I'm tough, too. I can lick my weight in wild flowers.

> W.C. Fields
> **The Big Broadcast of 1938** 1938

I was going to thrash them within an inch of their lives but I didn't have a tape measure.

> Groucho Marx
> **Go West** 1940

That's one of the tragedies of this life, that the men who are most in need of a beating up are always enormous.

Rudy Vallee
**The Palm Beach Story** 1942

— He's not as tough as he thinks.
— Neither are we.

Robert Redford and Paul Newman
**The Sting** 1973

— I don't know if I can lick you, or you can lick me, but I'll tell you one thing I do know.
— What?
— Together we can lick 'em all.

Spencer Tracy and Katharine Hepburn
**Pat and Mike** 1952

# HATE

Tell her I'd love to meet her. Tell her to wear boxing gloves.

> Irene Dunne
> **The Awful Truth** 1937

I don't like lobsters. I have a long list of dislikes. It's getting longer.

> Joan Crawford to Jeff Chandler
> **Female on the Beach** 1955

When a woman can love a man right down to her fingertips she can hate him the same way.

> Jean Harlow to Clark Gable
> **China Seas** 1935

— What do you call it when you hate the woman you love?
— A wife.

> Jack Lemmon and Terry-Thomas
> **How to Murder Your Wife** 1965

13

Everything you do irritates me. And when
you're not here, the things I know you're
gonna do when you come in irritate me.

> Walter Matthau to Jack Lemmon
> **The Odd Couple** 1968

We're not quarreling. We're in complete
agreement. We hate each other.

> Nanette Fabray about Oscar Levant
> **The Band Wagon** 1953

# INSULTS

— I've never been so insulted in all my life.
— Well, it's early yet.

> Esther Muir and Groucho Marx
> **A Day at the Races** 1937

What you are, I wouldn't eat.

> Felix Bressart as a Jewish actor to Lionel Atwill
> **To Be Or Not to Be** 1942

14

— You bastard!
— Yes sir. With me, an accident of birth. But you, you're a self-made man.

Ralph Bellamy and Lee Marvin
**The Professionals** 1966


— You make me sick.
— Well, use your own sink.

Charles McGraw and Marie Windsor
**The Narrow Margin** 1952


— Have you no human consideration?
— Show me a human and I might have.

Gary Merril and Bette Davis
**All About Eve** 1950


— May I come in?
— Oh, sure, I guess you'll be safe. The exterminators won't be here till tomorrow.

Gail Patrick and Ginger Rogers
**Stage Door** 1937

How is Tall, Dark and Obnoxious?

> Marjorie Davies to John Wayne
> **They Were Expendable** 1945

— You despise me, don't you?
— If I gave you any thought I probably would.

> Peter Lorre and Humphrey Bogart
> **Casablanca** 1942

I'd buy you a parachute if I thought it wouldn't open.

> Groucho Marx to Chico Marx
> **A Day at the Races** 1937

Why don't you bore a hole in yourself and let the sap run out?

> Groucho Marx to Chico Marx
> **Horse Feathers** 1932

I wouldn't go on living with you if you were dipped in platinum.

Irene Dunne to Cary Grant
**The Awful Truth** 1937


I need you as much as I need a giraffe.

William Powell to Jean Arthur
**The Ex-Mrs Bradford** 1936


You're like those carnival joints I used to work in...big, flash on the outside but on the inside nothing but filth.

Kirk Douglas to Lauren Bacall
**Young Man With a Horn** 1950


You sound like a very bad melodrama.

Glenn Ford
**Gilda** 1946

– Some people call me a wit.
– And they're half right.

Robert Woolsey and Bert Wheeler
**Caught Plastered** 1931

You must come down with me to the lumber-
yard and ride piggy-back on the buzz saw.

W.C. Fields
**You Can't Cheat an Honest Man** 1939

– Sir, you are no gentleman.
– And you, miss, are no lady.

Clark Gable and Vivien Leigh
**Gone With the Wind** 1939

There's a name for you ladies, but it isn't
used in high society – outside of a kennel.

Joan Crawford
**The Women** 1939

*Strange*? She's right out of *The Hound of the Baskervilles*.

Monty Woolley on Ruth Vivian
**The Man Who Came to Dinner** 1941

He has every characteristic of a dog except loyalty.

Henry Fonda
**The Best Man** 1964

If you don't mind my mentioning it, Father, I think you have a mind like a swamp.

Diana Lynn
**The Miracle of Morgan's Creek** 1944

You know, Sheridan, you have one great advantage over everyone else in the world. You've never had to meet Sheridan Whiteside.

Bette Davis about Monty Woolley
**The Man Who Came to Dinner** 1941

— He's got a lot of charm.
— He comes by it naturally. His father was a
snake.

> Ralph Bellamy and Rosalind Russell about Cary
> Grant
> **His Girl Friday** 1940

You have the touch of a love-starved cobra.

> Monty Woolley
> **The Man Who Came to Dinner** 1941

Your skin makes the Rocky Mountains look
like chiffon velvet.

> Peggy Shannon to Josephine Whittell
> **The Women** 1939

# COMPLIMENTS

— Oh, your Excellency!
— You're not so bad yourself.

> Margaret Dumont and Groucho Marx
> **Duck Soup** 1933

The arrangement of your features is not
entirely repulsive to me.

> Cyd Charisse to Fred Astaire
> **Silk Stockings** 1957

Those eyes, they're beautiful – and they
match.

> Bob Hope to Dorothy Lamour
> **Road to Utopia** 1945

What symmetrical digits!

> W.C. Fields to Mae West
> **My Little Chickadee** 1940

Oh, Walter, you're wonderful – in a
loathsome sort of way.

> Rosalind Russell to Cary Grant
> **His Girl Friday** 1940

You're a good man, sister.

> Humphrey Bogart pays his ultimate compliment to
> Lee Patrick
> **The Maltese Falcon** 1941

All other women are like the second pressing of the grape.

John Wayne to Susan Haywood
**The Conqueror** 1956

– Do you know what's wrong with you?
– No. What?
– Nothing.

Audrey Hepburn and Cary Grant
**Charade** 1963

# WORDPLAY

You're a French aristocrat, and she's a simple girl of the people, and she won't even give you a tumbrel.

Julius Tannen
**Singin' in the Rain** 1952

What do you mean illiterate? My mother and father were married at City Hall.

Joseph Downing
**Another Thin Man**  1939


I'm just a milestone around your neck.

Claudette Colbert to Joel McCrea
**The Palm Beach Story**  1942


– That's in every contract. It's what they call a sanity clause.
– You can't fool me.  There ain't no Sanity Clause.

Groucho Marx and Chico Marx
**A Night at the Opera**  1935


Remember the old adage: you can lead a horse to water, but a pencil must be lead.

Stan Laurel
**Brats**  1930

I'll send you an an onion. That'll make your
ice water.

Groucho Marx
**The Cocoanuts** 1929

The pellet with the poison's in the flagon
with the dragon. The vessel with the pestle
has the brew that is true.

Danny Kaye
**The Court Jester** 1956

I know. You know I know. I know you know I
know. We know Henry knows and Henry
knows we know. We're a knowledgeable
family.

Katharine Hepburn
**The Lion in Winter** 1968

What's a joint like this doing in a girl like
you?

Dean Martin about Kim Novak's knee
**Kiss Me, Stupid** 1964

Oh, why can't we break away from all this, just you and I, and lodge with my fleas in the hills – I mean, flee to my lodge in the hills.

Groucho Marx to Thelma Todd
**Monkey Business** 1931

Love flies out the door when money comes innuendo.

Groucho Marx
**Monkey Business** 1931

I hope all your teeth have cavities, and don't forget: abscess makes the heart grow fonder.

Groucho Marx
**The Cocoanuts** 1929

Time wounds all heels.

Groucho Marx
**Go West** 1940

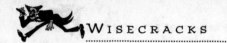

Anything further, father? That can't be
right. Isn't it, 'Anything father, further?'

Groucho Marx
**Horse Feathers** 1932

# NEWSPAPERS

You're a newspaperman. I can smell 'em. I've
always been able to smell 'em. Excuse me
while I open a window.

Charles Winninger
**Nothing Sacred** 1937

I can handle big news and little news, and if
there's no news, I'll go out and bite a dog.

Kirk Douglas
**Ace in the Hole** 1951

26

— Do you know what a sex maniac does?
— No.
— He sells newspapers.

Clark Gordon and Beau Bridges
**Gaily, Gaily** 1969

This time yesterday she was just another
pretty girl. Today she's the marmalade on
ten thousand pieces of toast.

Mark Hellinger
**The Naked City** 1948

Oh, I think you can always get people
interested in the crucifixion of a woman.

Aline MacMahon to editor, Edward G. Robinson
**Five Star Final** 1931

— Look Mr Carter, here is a three-column
headline in *The Chronicle*. Why hasn't *The
Inquirer* got a three-column headline?
— The news wasn't big enough.
— Mr Carter, if the headline is big enough it
makes the news big enough.

> Orson Welles and Erskine Sanford
> **Citizen Kane** 1941

Sentiment comes easy at fifty cents a word.

> Clifton Webb as a columnist
> **Laura** 1944

I'll tell you briefly what I think of
newspapermen: the hand of God reaching
down into the mire couldn't elevate one of
them to the depths of degradation — not by a
million miles.

> Charles Winninger
> **Nothing Sacred** 1937

– I got rid of all those reporters.
– What did you tell them?
– We're out of scotch.
– What a gruesome idea.

Myrna Loy and William Powell
**Another Thin Man** 1939

# GOODBYES

Hello. Is this someone with good news or
money? No? Goodbye.

Jason Robard giving good 'phone
**A Thousand Clowns** 1965

Nothing says goodbye like a bullet.

Elliott Gould
**The Long Goodbye** 1973

– I have a very pleasant surprise for you.
– How long will you be gone?

Walter Catlett and Charles Laughton
**It Started With Eve** 1941

— I really must be going. I'm usually in bed
at this hour.
— This must be one of your off-nights.

Mae West and Elizabeth Patterson
**Go West, Young Man** 1936

I shall repair to the bosom of my family — a
dismal place I admit.

W.C. Fields
**The Bank Dick** 1940

You go Uruguay and I'll go mine.

Groucho Marx
**Animal Crackers** 1930

And now will you all leave quietly, or must I
ask Miss Cutler to pass among you with a
baseball bat?

Monty Woolley
**The Man Who Came to Dinner** 1941

— Would you be good enough to shut the door?
— It's already shut.
— On your way out.

> Jean Harlow and Robert Taylor
> **Personal Property** 1937

— In other words, you're throwing me out.
— Not in other words. Those are the perfect words.

> Jack Lemmon and Walter Matthau
> **The Odd Couple** 1968

Come back when you can't stay so long.

> Aline MacMahon to William Warren
> **Gold Diggers of 1933** 1933

Go! And never darken my towels again.

> Groucho Marx
> **Duck Soup** 1933

31

If you're ever in New York, try and find me.

Monty Woolley<br>
**The Man Who Came to Dinner** 1941

Goodbye, thanks for calling. If you ever need a good pallbearer, remember, I'm at your service.

Ginger Rogers to Gail Patrick<br>
**Stage Door** 1937

Goodbye, and don't think it hasn't been a little slice of heaven, 'cause it hasn't.

Bugs Bunny<br>
**Hair-Raising Hare** 1946

– Where is Mr Hardy?
– He's right here, and he told me to tell you that we just left – ten minutes ago.

James Finlayson on the 'phone to Stan Laurel<br>
**Me and My Pal** 1933

# APPEARANCE

# GENERAL

– I saw your face in the wings. Made me feel
I was doing everything wrong.
– I got that kind of face.

> Joan Crawford and Clark Gable
> **Dancing Lady** 1933

– You're not very tall, are you?
– I try to be.

> Martha Vickers and Humphrey Bogart
> **The Big Sleep** 1946

– You're a mess, aren't you?
– I'm not very tall, either. Next time I'll come
on stilts.

> Lauren Bacall and Humphrey Bogart
> **The Big Sleep** 1946

– How tall are you without your horse?
– Well, ma'am, I'm six feet seven inches.
– Never mind the six feet, let's talk about the
seven inches.

Mae West and Cowboy Stud
**Myra Breckenridge** 1970

Is she standing in a hole?

W.C. Fields about diminutive Heather Wilde
**The Bank Dick** 1940

– What you need is a good bodyguard.
– What I need is a good body. The one I've
got isn't worth guarding.

Chico Marx and Groucho Marx
**A Night in Casablanca** 1946

Your eyes, your eyes...they shine like the
pants in my blue serge suit.

Groucho Marx
**The Cocoanuts** 1929

35

– Your eyes remind me of...
– Yes, yes, I know. Sparkling diamonds...deep sapphires...
– No...no. They remind me of...angry marbles.

> William Powell and Myrna Loy
> **Libeled Lady** 1936

Are you eating a tomato or is that your nose?

> Charlie McCarthy to W.C. Fields
> **You Can't Cheat an Honest Man** 1939

When it bleeds...the Red Sea!

> José Ferrer about his outsized nose
> **Cyrano de Bergerac** 1950

She was a charming middle-aged lady with a face like a bucket of mud.

> Dick Powell
> **Murder, My Sweet** 1944

Any resemblance between these two
characters and living persons is purely
coincidental.

> Groucho Marx about Chico and Harpo
> **Go West** 1940

Well, don't stand there, Miss Preen. You look
like frozen custard.

> Monty Woolley
> **The Man Who Came to Dinner** 1941

# BEAUTY

I don't especially like the way I look sometimes, but I never met a man since I was 14
that didn't want to give me an argument
about it.

> Lana Turner
> **The Postman Always Rings Twice** 1946

– Is she prettier than me?
– Is she prettier than you? *I'm* prettier than
you.

> Edra Gale and Peter Sellers
> **What's New Pussycat?** 1965

You're one of the most beautiful women I've
ever seen and that's not saying much for
you.

> Groucho Marx to Margaret Dumont
> **Animal Crackers** 1930

I don't know what you'll look like tomorrow,
but right now, baby, you're the most beautiful dame in the world.

> Clark Gable to Joan Crawford
> **Strange Cargo** 1940

When I get through with you, you'll look
like...well, what do you call beautiful? A
tree? You'll look like a tree.

> Fred Astaire to Audrey Hepburn
> **Funny Face** 1956

38

– Beauty is only skin deep.
– That's deep enough for me.

> Bud Abbott and Lou Costello
> **Rio Rita** 1942

With a binding like you've got, people are
going to want to know what's in the book.

> Gene Kelly to Leslie Caron
> **An American in Paris** 1951

They say that Elizabeth surrounds herself
with beauty in the hope that it may be
contagious.

> Claude Rains
> **The Sea Hawk** 1940

Just a moment, Miss Jones, I've been very
curious about something for years. Let your
hair down... Now take your glasses off...
Strange, always seems to work in the movies.

> Gig Young finding his secretary is not a dish after all
> **That Touch of Mink** 1962

Even I cannot make a peach melba out of a prune.

> George K. Arthur to Colleen Moore
> **Irene** 1926

Daylight has never exposed so total a ruin.

> Vivien Leigh looking in a mirror
> **A Streetcar Named Desire** 1951

He makes Frankenstein look like a lily.

> Glenda Farrell
> **The Mystery of the Wax Museum** 1933

Love means never having to say you're ugly.

> Vincent Price
> **The Abominable Dr Phibes** 1971

My Great Aunt Jennifer ate a whole box of candy every day of her life. She lived to be 102, and when she had been dead three days, she looked better than you do now.

> Monty Woolley to Mary Wickes
> **The Man Who Came to Dinner** 1941

# HAIR

— You know, you'd be very beautiful with
blonde hair.
— I *have* blonde hair.
— I know.

Fred MacMurray and Carole Lombard
**Hands Across the Table** 1935


— You don't look like a man who'd be
interested in first editions.
— I collect blondes in bottles, too.

Carole Douglas and Humphrey Bogart
**The Big Sleep** 1946


I was in love with a beautiful blonde once.
She drove me to drink. That's the one thing
I'm indebted to her for.

W.C. Fields
**Never Give a Sucker an Even Break** 1941

Just because he prefers blondes doesn't make him a gentleman.

Leon Erroll
**Mexican Spitfire's Blessed Event** 1943


I hate big league blondes. All bubble-bath and dewy morning and moonlight. And inside, blue steel...cold, cold...only not so clean.

Anne Shirley
**Murder, My Sweet** 1944


In my time, women with hair like that didn't come outside in the daylight.

Elizabeth Patterson to Mae West
**Go West, Young Man** 1936


– Are you asking for a lock of my hair?
– I'm letting you off lightly. I was going to ask for the whole wig.

Margaret Dumont and Groucho Marx
(Margaret Dumont really was bald)
**Duck Soup** 1933

I'm a flaming redhead. If you play with fire, you'll get burned.

Ann Sheridan
**Take Me To Town** 1953


— There's a man outside with a big black moustache.
— Tell him I've got one.

Chico Marx and Groucho Marx
**Horse Feathers** 1932


Don't point that beard at me, it might go off.

Groucho Marx
**A Day at the Races** 1937


You're the only man in the world with clenched hair.

Walter Matthau about uptight Jack Lemmon
**The Odd Couple** 1968


43

# DRESS

– Can you see through this dress?
– I'm afraid you can, miss.
– I'll wear it.

> Jean Harlow and Sales Assistant
> **Red-headed Woman** 1932

– May I suggest, if you're dressing to please
Stephen, not *that* one. He doesn't like such
obvious effects.
– Thanks for the tip, but when anything I
wear doesn't please Stephen, I take it off.

> Norma Shearer and Joan Crawford
> **The Women** 1939

– I'll finish dressing.
– Oh, please, don't. Not on my account.

> Jill St John and Sean Connery
> **Diamonds are Forever** 1971

44

I like a girl in a bikini...no concealed
weapons.

> Roger Moore
> **The Man With the Golden Gun** 1974

Would you be shocked if I put on something
more comfortable?

> Jean Harlow to Ben Lyon
> **Hell's Angels** 1930

– That's quite a dress you almost have on.
What holds it up?
– Modesty.

> Gene Kelly and Nina Foch
> **An American in Paris** 1951

For a dress like that you gotta start laying
plans when you're about 13.

> Jean Peters about Marilyn Monroe's figure hugging
> dress
> **Niagara** 1953

45

How did you get into that dress – with a spray gun?

Bob Hope to Dorothy Lamour
**Road to Rio** 1947

I can never get a zipper to close. Maybe that stands for something, what do you think?

Rita Hayworth
**Gilda** 1946

– Well, you son of a sea snake. Have you got on my new pajamas? You shake right out of them, Hortense. I'm too important to sleep informally. What if there'd be a fire?
– You'd have to cover up to keep from being recognised.

Jean Harlow and Una Merkel
**Red-headed Woman** 1932

She pulled her skirt down over her knees as if they were a national treasure.

Martin Gabel about Tippi Hedren
**Marnie** 1964

46

Oh, I think that dress is a dream on you. You know, it does something to your face. It... it gives you a chin.

Mary Astor
**Midnight** 1939


I hate this dress. My husband says I look as though I were going to sing in it.

Phyllis Povah
**The Women** 1939


The morning after always does look grim if you happen to be wearing last night's dress.

Ina Claire to Greta Garbo
**Ninotchka** 1939


I think it's very unselfish of those little animals to give up their lives to keep other animals warm.

Ginger Rogers to Gail Patrick in a fur coat
**Stage Door** 1937


47

You may as well go to perdition in ermine.
You're sure to come back in rags.

Katharine Hepburn loaning her fur to Ginger Rogers
**Stage Door** 1937


— Why are you wearing these clothes?
— Because I just went gay all of a sudden!

May Robson to Cary Grant in a fluffy negligée
**Bringing Up Baby** 1938


I can afford a blemish on my character but
not on my clothes.

Vincent Price
**Laura** 1944


It's been four years since I saw you, but I
recognize the suit.

Lucille Ball to Bob Hope
**Sorrowful Jones** 1949

Burn his suits. Even the moths wouldn't eat them.

Maude Eburne
**Ruggles of Red Gap** 1935


Morals never bothered me much but taste is so important.

Douglas Fairbanks Jr.
**Scarlet Dawn** 1932


Nobody wears a beige suit to a bank robbery.

Woody Allen
**Take the Money and Run** 1969


And another thing. Please promise me never to wear black satin, or pearls, or to be 36 years old.

Laurence Olivier to Joan Fontaine
**Rebecca** 1940

# JEWELRY

— Goodness, what beautiful diamonds.
— Goodness had nothing to do with it, dearie.

Cloakroom Girl and Mae West
**Night After Night** 1932

It was a toss up whether I go in for
diamonds or sing in the choir. The choir lost.

Mae West
**She Done Him Wrong** 1933

I always say a kiss on the hand might feel
very good, but a diamond tiara lasts forever.

Marilyn Monroe
**Gentlemen Prefer Blondes** 1953

I just love finding new places to wear
diamonds.

Marilyn Monroe
**Gentlemen Prefer Blondes** 1953

Of course, personally, I think it'd be tacky to wear diamonds before I'm 40.

Audrey Hepburn
**Breakfast at Tiffany's** 1961

It doesn't matter who gives them as long as you never wear anything second-rate. Wait for the first-class jewels, Gigi. Hold on to your ideals.

Isabel Jeans
**Gigi** 1958

Real diamonds! They must be worth their weight in gold.

Marilyn Monroe
**Some Like It Hot** 1959

This is just mah summer jewelry. You oughtta see mah winter stuff.

Mae West
**She Done Him Wrong** 1933

I can recommend the bait. I ought to know –
I bit on it myself.

> Tallulah Bankhead offering her diamonds as bait
> **Lifeboat** 1944

# LOOKS

I killed a guy for looking at me the way you
are now.

> Humphrey Bogart
> **Dead End** 1937

He looks as if he knows what I look like
without my shimmy.

> Vivien Leigh about Clark Gable
> **Gone With the Wind** 1939

You've got that look, that look that leaves me
weak, you with your eyes-across-the-table
technique.

> Marlene Dietrich
> **Destry Rides Again** 1938

52

It's better to be looked over than overlooked.

Mae West
**Belle of the Nineties** 1934

She threw me a look I caught in my hip
pocket.

Robert Mitchum
**Farewell, My Lovely** 1975

— I feel like everybody's staring at me.
— With those legs, are you crazy?

Jack Lemmon and Tony Curtis, both in drag
**Some Like It Hot** 1959

# THE BODY

# FOOD

I want a sit-down orgy for 40.

Leon Green
**A Funny Thing Happened On the Way To the Forum**
1966


Do you want a leg or a breast?

Grace Kelly offering cold chicken to Cary Grant on a
picnic
**To Catch a Thief** 1955


The picnic is off. We don't have any red ants.

Groucho Marx
**Monkey Business** 1931


Watercress! I'd just as soon eat my way
across a front lawn.

Phyllis Povah
**The Women** 1939

Beulah, peel me a grape.

Mae West
**I'm No Angel** 1933

Have caviar if you like, but it tastes like
herring to me.

Joan Crawford
**Grand Hotel** 1932

Waiter, will you serve the nuts – I mean,
would you serve the guests the nuts?

Myrna Loy
**The Thin Man** 1934

Dunking's an art. Don't let it soak so long. A
dip, and pop into your mouth. If you let it
hang there too long, it'll get soft and fall off.
It's all a matter of timing.

Clark Gable dunking doughnuts with Claudette
Colbert
**It Happened One Night** 1934

— I could go for a dish of ice cream.
— We haven't got any ice cream.
— Well, you could go and get some ice cream.
— Get me my new hat, and I'll go and get some ice cream.
— You going to get it in your hat?

> Stan Laurel and Oliver Hardy
> **Come Clean** 1931

— There's a fly in my ice cream.
— The flies here go in for winter sports.

> Patsy Kelly and Bert Lahr
> **Sing Your Worries Away** 1942

— I got brown sandwiches and green sandwiches. Which one do you want?
— What's the green?
— It's either very new cheese or very old meat.
— I'll take the brown.

> Walter Matthau and Herb Edelman
> **The Odd Couple** 1968

I didn't squawk about the steak, dear. I
merely said I didn't see that old horse that
used to be tethered outside.

W.C. Fields
**Never Give a Sucker an Even Break** 1941

– I can cook. I'm a terrific cook.
– You don't have to cook. I've got enough
potato chips to last me a year.

Jack Lemmon and Walter Matthau
**The Odd Couple** 1968

– Freddie Hope has got pneumonia, on the
day of my dinner party, too. What am I
going to do?
– Why do anything? I never could
understand why it had to be just even, male
and female. They're invited for dinner, not
mating.

Billie Burke and May Robson
**Dinner at Eight** 1933

You call this a party? The beer is warm, the
women are cold, and I'm hot under the
collar. In fact, a more poisonous barbecue
I've never attended.

> Groucho Marx
> **Monkey Business** 1931

# DRINK

Let's get something to eat. I'm thirsty.

> William Powell
> **After The Thin Man** 1936

Some weasel took the cork out of my lunch.

> W.C. Fields
> **You Can't Cheat an Honest Man** 1939

— Do you think he drinks?
— Well, he didn't get that nose from playing
ping-pong.

> Susan Miller and Margaret Dumont about W.C. Fields
> **Never Give a Sucker an Even Break** 1941

60

— Why does she drink? There must be a reason.
— There is. She likes it.

> Taina Elg and Mitzi Gaynor about Kay Kendall
> **Les Girls**  1957

— What are you trying to do, drown your troubles?
— No, I'm just teaching them to swim.

> Stanley Adams and Bob Hope
> **Critic's Choice**  1963

— Was I in here last night, and did I spend a 20 dollar bill?
— Yeah.
— Oh boy, what a load that is off my mind. I thought I'd lost it.

> W.C. Fields and Bartender
> **The Bank Dick**  1940

I shall look for the answer tonight at the bottom of a large rum and coke.

Vincent Price
**The Eve of St. Mark** 1944

Gin was mother's milk to her.

Audrey Hepburn about her aunt
**My Fair Lady** 1964

With Guzzler's Gin, you don't need a chaser. Nothing can catch you.

Red Skelton
**Ziegfeld Follies** 1946

The important thing is the rhythm. You should always have rhythm in your shaking. Now a Manhattan you shake to a fox trot; a Bronx to a two-step time. A dry martini you always shake to waltz time.

William Powell
**The Thin Man** 1934

– Whiskey is slow poison.
– So who's in a hurry?

Fred Allen and Robert Benchley
**It's in the Bag** 1945

– Will you join me in a glass of wine?
– You get in first, and if there's room
enough, I'll join you.

Peggy Hopkins Joyce and W.C. Fields
**International House** 1933

Was I a good year?

Zero Mostel
**A Funny Thing Happened On the Way to the Forum**
1966

I never drink...wine.

Bela Lugosi
**Dracula** 1931

I think you'll enjoy this. Type Double O
Positive.  A rare type.

Alex D'Arcy
**Blood of Dracula's Castle**  1969

Have a drink – just a little one to lessen the
difference in our characters.

Noel Coward
**The Scoundrel**  1935

– I'll have the usual – bourbon and water.
– You were all out of bourbon, so I made it
straight water.

Woody Allen and Diane Keaton
**Play it Again, Sam**  1972

I'll take a lemonade – in a dirty glass.

Bob Hope being mucho macho
**Road to Utopia**  1945

– One beer, please.
– And two clean straws that haven't been used.

> Oliver Hardy and Stan Laurel
> **Pack Up Your Troubles** 1932


– How do you like your brandy, sir?
– In a glass.

> Charles Waldron and Humphrey Bogart
> **The Big Sleep** 1946


Don't put any ice in mine. Takes up too much room.

> Groucho Marx
> **Go West** 1940


– You drank it all! We were supposed to share it.
– I couldn't help it. My half was on the bottom.

> Oliver Hardy and Stan Laurel
> **Men o' War** 1929

During one of our trips through Afghanistan,
we lost our corkscrew. We had to live on
food and water for several days.

W.C. Fields
**My Little Chickadee** 1940


I don't know what I'm doing here when I
could be at home in bed with a hot toddy.
That's a drink.

Groucho Marx
**At the Circus** 1939


– Have you ever seen a flying saucer?
– Is that your way of offering me a drink?

James Gregory and Dean Martin
**The Ambushers** 1967


I'd like to ask you to stay and have a drink,
but I'm afraid you might accept.

Joan Crawford being less than neighborly to Jeff
Chandler
**Female on the Beach** 1955


66

– Can I buy you a drink?
– No, thanks, I don't drink, but I'll take the
money instead.

Barfly and Huntz Hall
**In the Money** 1958

– Could you be persuaded to have a drink,
dear?
– Well, maybe just a tiny triple.

Lucille Ball
**Mame** 1974

I've been drinking over 40 years, and I
haven't acquired the habit yet.

Guy Kibbee
**Joy of Living** 1938

They may be drinkers, Robin, but they're still
human beings.

Adam West to Burt Ward
**Batman** 1966

There comes a time in every woman's life when the only thing that helps is a glass of champagne.

Bette Davis
**Old Acquaintance** 1943

Champagne. I love it. It tastes like your foot's asleep.

Joan Davis
**George White's Sandals** 1945

— Hmm, domestic and terribly flat.
— That's the water.

Bob Hope and Fred Clark
**Here Come the Girls** 1953

Champagne is a great levelerer — leveler. It makes you my equal.

James Stewart to Cary Grant
**The Philadelphia Story** 1940

He's so full of alcohol, if you put a lighted
wick in his mouth he'd burn for three days.

Groucho Marx
Go West 1940

— You're drunk.
— Yeah, and you're crazy. I'll be sober
tomorrow, but you'll be crazy the rest of
your life.

Kathleen Howard and W.C. Fields
It's a Gift 1934

In the event of drunkenness — mine, not
yours — I shall ask a depth of understanding
one may expect only from a child.

Frank Morgan to Mickey Rooney
The Human Comedy 1943

# HANGOVER

Gaaad, what a night! I'll never mix radish
juice and carrot juice again.

> Bugs Bunny
> **Hare-Way to the Stars** 1958

Somebody put too many olives in my
martinis last night.

> W.C. Fields
> **Never Give a Sucker an Even Break** 1941

I've had hangovers before, but this time even
my hair hurts.

> Rock Hudson
> **Pillow Talk** 1959

I feel as though the Russian army has been
walking over my tongue in their stockinged
feet.

> W.C. Fields
> **Six of a Kind** 1934

I'm testing the air. I like it, but it doesn't like me.

James Stewart surfacing after a hangover
**The Philadelphia Story** 1940


This is one of those days which the pages of history teach us are best spent lying in bed.

Roland Young
**The Philadelphia Story** 1940


I envy people who drink. At least they know what to blame everything on.

Oscar Levant
**Humoresque** 1947


# VICES

– Too many girls follow the line of least resistance.
– Yes, but a good line is hard to resist.

Helen Jerome Eddy and Mae West
**Klondike Annie** 1936

When I'm caught between two evils, I
generally like to take the one I never tried.

Mae West
**Klondike Annie** 1936


— How about a little gin rummy?
— I don't drink, thank you. Never touch it.

William Demarest and Torben Meyer
**Sullivan's Travels** 1941


Take a card. You can keep it. I still have 51
left.

Groucho Marx
**Duck Soup** 1933


— Is this a game of chance?
— Not the way I play it.

Fuzzy Knight and W.C. Fields
**My Little Chickadee** 1940

– These dice ain't got no spots on 'em.
They're blank.
– I had the spots removed for luck, but I
remember where the spots formerly were.

> Frank Sinatra and B.S. Pully
> **Guys and Dolls** 1955

See that chess game over there? When I was
four years old, I played ten people all at once
– blindfolded. I lost every game.

> Robert Benchley
> **China Seas** 1935

– Is there a way to win?
– There's a way to lose more slowly.

> Jane Greer and Robert Mitchum
> **Build My Gallows High** 1947

Don't forget Lady Godiva put everything she
had on a horse.

> W.C. Fields
> **Tillie and Gus** 1933

— Would you like to buy a raffle ticket for the
church for fifty cents?
— Now what would I do with a church if I
won one?

Little Boy and Jackie Gleason
**Papa's Delicate Condition** 1963

I never smoked a cigarette until I was nine.

W.C. Fields
**The Bank Dick** 1940

Cigarette me, big boy.

Barbara Stanwyck
**Young Man of Manhattan** 1930

— Cigarette?
— No, thanks, gave it up when I was seven.

William Corson and Ginger Rogers
**Stage Door** 1937

# SPORTS

Boxing is the only sport in the world where
two guys get paid for doing something
they'd be arrested for if they got drunk and
did it for nothing.

Paul Stewart
**Champion** 1949

The only arithmetic he ever got was hearing
the referee count up to ten.

Rod Steiger about Marlon Brando
**On the Waterfront** 1954

– Water polo? Isn't that terribly dangerous?
– I'll say! I had two ponies drowned under
me.

Marilyn Monroe and Tony Curtis
**Some Like It Hot** 1959

We're neglecting football for education.

Groucho Marx
**Horse Feathers** 1932

– Must you wear glasses?
– Oh, no, sir. Only when I want to see.

Football Coach and Jerry Lewis
**That's My Boy** 1951

– Many an afternoon, we had tea, the
Duchess and I, while her husband, the Duke,
was busily engaged in his favorite sport.
– Was that cricket?
– Perhaps not, but she was irresistible.

Bob Hope and Percy Helton
**Fancy Pants** 1950

# DIET

– Gaining a little weight aren't you, honey?
– You're no cream puff yourself, dearie.

Two Performing Elephants
**Dumbo** 1941

— You're gaining weight.
— Yes, I'll soon be your size.

Geneva Mitchell and Mary Duncan
**Morning Glory** 1933

I can see you now, bending over a hot
stove...only I can't see the stove.

Groucho Marx to Margaret Dumont
**The Cocoanuts** 1929

In the water, I'm a very skinny lady.

Shelley Winters
**The Poseidon Adventure** 1972

Do I look heavyish to you? I feel heavyish.
Put a note on my desk in the morning,
'Think thin'.

Cary Grant to his secretary
**North by Northwest** 1959

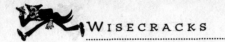

The only exercise you ever get is jumping to conclusions.

Danny Kaye
**The Secret Life of Walter Mitty** 1947

– Look at that paunch. You ought to diet.
– But I like it this color.

Wally Brown and Alan Carney
**Adventures of a Rookie** 1943

Nobody loves a fat man, except his grocer and his tailor.

Charles McGraw
**The Narrow Margin** 1952

# HEALTH

– Could you go for a doctor?
– Sure! Send him in.

Rita Orwin and Myrna Loy
**Love Me Tonight** 1932

Dr Bradley is the greatest living argument
for mercy killings.

Monty Woolley
**The Man Who Came to Dinner** 1941

Go in and read the life of Florence
Nightingale and learn how unfitted you are
for your chosen profession.

Monty Woolley to Mary Wickes as a nurse
**The Man Who Came to Dinner** 1941

Insomnia? I know a good cure for it...get
plenty of sleep.

W.C. Fields
**Never Give a Sucker an Even Break** 1941

– The doctor thinks that my cold might be
caused by psychology.
– Naah, how does he know you got
psychology?

Vivian Blaine and Frank Sinatra
**Guys and Dolls** 1955

T.B. or not T.B., that is the congestion.

Woody Allen
**Everything You Always Wanted to Know About Sex (But Were Afraid to Ask)** 1972

A thrill a day keeps the chill away.

Mae West
**Go West, Young Man** 1936

# AGE

Old age. It's the only disease that you don't look forward to being cured of.

Everett Sloane
**Citizen Kane** 1941

You still have your hourglass figure, my dear, but most of the sand has gone to the bottom.

Bob Hope
**The Lemon Drop Kid** 1950

I'd like to give you some encouragement, but all I can say is, Chins up.

Charles Coburn
**Heaven Can Wait** 1943

Bill's 32. He looks 32. He looked it 5 years ago. He'll look it 20 years from now. I hate men.

Bette Davis
**All About Eve** 1950

I like older men. They're so grateful.

Greta Garbo
**Two-Faced Woman** 1941

He's 40, which means he'll consider any female over 18 too old.

Agnes Moorhead
**All That Heaven Allows** 1955

– How many people in the world over 40 can
still say they have all their own teeth?
– How many people over 50 can still say
they're only 40?

Victor Mature and Martin Balsam
After the Fox 1966

# LIFE

Life is a banquet, and most poor suckers are
starving to death.

Rosalind Russell
Auntie Mame 1958

This is a story of passion, bloodshed, desire
and death, everything, in fact, that makes
life worth living.

Prologue
Irma La Douce 1963

— For a long time I was ashamed of the way I lived.
— You mean to say you reformed?
— No, I got over being ashamed.

Mae West and Paul Cavanagh
**Goin' to Town** 1935

I don't have a lifestyle. I have a life.

Jane Fonda
**California Suite** 1978

Isn't it wonderful to see all our lives so settled...temporarily?

Mary Boland
**The Women** 1939

Once again, life louses up the script.

Humphrey Bogart
**The Barefoot Contessa** 1954

That's all we are – amateurs. We don't live
long enough to be anything else.

> Charlie Chaplin
> **Limelight** 1952


– Shall I kill myself?
– Don't minimize this.

> Glenn Ford and Paul Ford
> **The Teahouse of the August Moon** 1956


He won't kill himself. It'd please too many
people.

> Roscoe Karns
> **Twentieth Century** 1934


He's too nervous to kill himself. He wears his
seatbelt in a drive-in movie.

> Walter Matthau about Jack Lemmon
> **The Odd Couple** 1968

Man is the only animal clever enough to build the Empire State Building and stupid enough to jump off it.

Rock Hudson
**Come September** 1961

It's a funny old life...man's lucky if he gets out of it alive.

W.C. Fields
**You're Telling Me** 1934

# DEATH

Either he's dead or my watch has stopped.

Groucho Marx
**A Day at the Races** 1937

I fell asleep without realizing it. When I was awakened, there were my relatives, saying nothing but the kindest things about me. Then I knew I was dead.

Don Ameche in spirit form
**Heaven Can Wait** 1943

— Is it true that my dear, dear daddy is dead?
— I hope so. They buried him.

Rosina Lawrence and Stan Laurel
**Way Out West** 1937

— I'm sorry to hear that. It must be hard to lose your mother-in-law.
— Yes, it is, very hard, almost imposs– oh yes.

Carlotta Monti and W.C. Fields
**Man on the Flying Trapeze** 1935

— My uncle fell through a trap door and
broke his neck.
— Was he building a house?
— No, they were hanging him.

Stan Laurel and Oliver Hardy
**The Laurel and Hardy Murder Case** 1930


— Not the guillotine?
— Be brave, my friend. You wanted to die,
anyway.
— But like a man, not a salami.

Bob Hope and Patric Knowles
**Monsieur Beaucaire** 1946


It's like sittin' in a barber chair. They're
gonna ask me, 'You got anything to say?'
and I say, 'Sure. Give me a haircut, a shave
and a massage — one of those nice new
electrical massages.'

James Cagney
**Angels With Dirty Faces** 1938

If I get the electric chair my agent gets ten
per cent of the current.

Bob Hope
**My Favorite Blonde** 1942


— Someday you'll drown in a vat of whiskey.
— Drown in a vat of whiskey. Death, where is
thy sting?

Carlotta Monti and W.C. Fields
**Never Give a Sucker an Even Break** 1941

# PEOPLE AND
# RELATIONSHIPS

# MEN

Sometimes you wonder what God had in mind when he invented the male sex.

Rita Hayworth
**Fire Down Below**  1957

– There are only two perfectly good men –
one dead, the other unborn.
– Which one are you?

Harold Huber and Mae West
**Klondike Annie**  1936

The only difference between men is the color of their ties.

Helen Broderick
**Top Hat**  1935

– What kind of men do you like?
– Just two, domestic and imported.

John Miljan and Mae West
**Belle of the Nineties**  1934

90

Some men just naturally make you think of brut champagne. With others, you think of prune juice.

Barbara Lawrence
**Unfaithfully Yours** 1948

Jonathan is more than a man. He's an experience, and he's habit-forming. If they could ever bottle him, he'd outsell ginger ale.

Barry Sullivan about Kirk Douglas
**The Bad and the Beautiful** 1952

– Promise me you'll never think of another man.
– That depends on you.

Roger Pryor and Mae West
**Belle of the Nineties** 1934

If there's one thing I know, it's men. I ought to. It's been my life's work.

Marie Dressler
**Dinner at Eight** 1933

It's not the men in my life that counts – it's
the life in my men.

Mae West
**I'm No Angel** 1933

# WOMEN

– I wonder what kind of woman you are?
– Too bad I don't give out samples.

Joseph Calleia and Mae West
**My Little Chickadee** 1940

I'm just an old-fashioned home girl. Like
Mae West.

Patsy Kelly
**The Girl From Missouri** 1934

Maybe she was all right – and maybe
Christmas comes in July. But I didn't believe
it.

Humphrey Bogart about Lizabeth Scott
**Dead Reckoning** 1947

– You're a dangerous woman.
– Thanks. You look good to me, too.

Paul Cavanagh and Mae West
**Goin' to Town** 1935

Women are like elephants. I like to watch
them, but I wouldn't want to own one.

W.C. Fields
**Mississippi** 1935

How extravagant you are, throwing away
women like that. Someday they may be
scarce.

Claude Rains to Humphrey Bogart
**Casablanca** 1942

Statistics show that there are more women in
the world than anything else – except
insects.

Glenn Ford
**Gilda** 1946

— Why do so many marriages go on the rocks?
— Because women are such lying, scheming, deceitful, mercenary hellcats?

> Dennis O'Keefe and Edward Everett Horton
> **Weekend For Three** 1941

— He treats her like she's one of the family.
— Is that good?

> Geraldine Wall and Frank Sinatra
> **Some Came Running** 1958

Women should be kept illiterate and clean, like canaries.

> Roscoe Karns
> **Woman of the Year** 1942

One woman should not judge another. She hasn't the glands for it.

> Peter Ustinov
> **Quo Vadis** 1951

I can tell you what an Indian will do to you,
but not a woman.

Gary Cooper
**The Plainsman** 1937

I'm old-fashioned. I like two sexes.

Spencer Tracy
**Adam's Rib** 1949

As the French say, 'Vive la différence!'
Which means, 'Hurray for that little
difference!'

Spencer Tracy
**Adam's Rib** 1949

# FLOOZIES

Lulubelle, it's you! I didn't recognize you
standing up.

Groucho Marx
**Go West** 1940

95

WISECRACKS

I'm sorry, I never remember a face.

> Shirley MacLaine to Jack Lemmon
> **Irma La Douce** 1963

— You remember Anne.
— Not Anytime Annie! Say, who could forget her? She only said 'no' once and then she didn't hear the question.

Una Merkel and George E. Stone about Ginger Rogers
**42nd Street** 1933

I used to make obscene phone calls to her, collect, and she used to accept the charges all the time.

> Woody Allen
> **Take the Money and Run** 1969

I'm no angel, but I've spread my wings a bit.

> Mae West
> **I'm No Angel** 1933

96

— I been under the impression that you is a one man woman.
— I am. One man at a time.

Libby Taylor and Mae West
**I'm No Angel** 1933

Armies have marched over me.

Rita Hayworth
**Fire Down Below** 1957

— A fine woman.
— One of the finest women that ever walked the streets.

Aggie Herring and Mae West
**She Done Him Wrong** 1933

I've been things and seen places.

Mae West
**She Done Him Wrong** 1933

If I'd been a ranch, they would've named me
the Bar Nothing.

Rita Hayworth
**Gilda** 1946

I started with Amherst and worked my way
through the alphabet to Yale. I'm stuck there.
'Course, I could work backwards again.

Elizabeth Taylor
**Butterfield 8** 1960

Available? You're like an old coat that's
hanging in the closet. Every time he reaches
in, there you are.

Joan Blondell to Katharine Hepburn
**Desk Set** 1957

I've been on more laps than a napkin.

Mae West
**I'm No Angel** 1933

She tried to sit on my lap while I was
standing up.

> Humphrey Bogart about Martha Vickers
> **The Big Sleep** 1946

# ATTRACTION

– I hear she's a dish.
– She's the 60-cent special.
– Cheap, flashy, strictly poison under the
gravy.

> Charles McGraw and Gus Forbes
> **The Narrow Margin** 1952

Hey, get out the fire-hose!

> Max Showalter spotting Marilyn Monroe
> **Niagara** 1953

She has eyes that men adore so, and a torso
even more so.

> Groucho Marx
> **At the Circus** 1939

I would sell my mother to the Arabs for her.

Woody Allen
**Play it Again, Sam** 1972

— You will meet a nice American woman who
will have much more than I have.
— I don't know where she'd put it.

Gina Lollobrigida and Bob Hope
**The Private Navy of Sgt. O'Farrell** 1968

She's nicely packed. Not much meat on her,
but what there is is *cherce*.

Spencer Tracy in his thick Brooklyn accent about
Katharine Hepburn
**Pat and Mike** 1952

Whether you're born with it, or catch it from
a public drinking cup, Maria had it.

Humphrey Bogart about Ava Gardner
**The Barefoot Contessa** 1964

100

I've seen women I'd look at quicker but never one I'd look at longer.

Clark Gable to Lana Turner
**Honky Tonk** 1941

Your knees in action – that's the attraction.

Dick Powell
**Dames** 1933

– Do you find me undesirable?
– Oh, no, Mrs Robinson. I think...I think you're the most attractive of all my parents' friends. I mean that.

Anne Bancroft and Dustin Hoffman
**The Graduate** 1967

In moments of quiet, I'm strangely drawn towards you, but...well, there haven't been any quiet moments.

Cary Grant to Katharine Hepburn
**Bringing Up Baby** 1938

— I've always looked for someone like you.
— Like me, eh? I'm not good enough?

Eve Arden and Groucho Marx
**At the Circus** 1939

I liked you 'cause I thought you had some feeling, but when you didn't, I liked you even more.

Mae West
**Go West, Young Man** 1936

— With you, I'm dynamite.
— Yeah, and I'm your match.

Fred Kohler and Mae West
**Goin' to Town** 1935

Those girls are all air-conditioned. Forty degrees cooler in the house than on the street.

Eddie Bracken
**Too Many Girls** 1940

I guess you are sort of attractive, in a
corn-fed sort of way. You can find yourself a
poor girl falling for you if...well, if you threw
in a set of dishes.

Bette Davis
**The Man Who Came to Dinner** 1941

— You know I've been mad about you from
the first time I laid eyes on you. Why, you're
my whole world. What do you want to do,
drive me to a madhouse?
— No, I'll call you a taxi.

George Raft and Mae West
**Night After Night** 1934

You have a very naughty mind, Ah'm happy
to say.

Gloria Grahame to Dick Powell
**The Bad and the Beautiful** 1952

# PROPOSITIONS

Whyncha come up sometime, 'n' see me?

> Mae West to Cary Grant
> **She Done Him Wrong** 1933

Anytime you got nothin' to do and lots of time t' do it...come up.

> Mae West to Joseph Calleia
> **My Little Chickadee** 1940

– What are you doing in the closet?
– Nothing.  Come on in.

> Thelma Todd and Groucho Marx
> **Monkey Business** 1931

Won't you come in for a moment? I don't bite, you know – unless it's called for.

> Audrey Hepburn to Cary Grant
> **Charade** 1963

Come on, darling. Why don't you kick off
your spurs?

Elizabeth Taylor to Rock Hudson
**Giant** 1956

Say, honey, you and me could make music
together and right now I feel like the
Philharmonic.

Bob Hope
**My Favorite Blonde** 1942

Meet me in the bedroom in five minutes, and
bring a cattle-prod.

Tatsuya Mihashi
**What's Up, Tiger Lily?** 1966

— Will I *see* you tonight?
— I never make plans so far in advance.

Madelaine LeBeau and Humphrey Bogart
**Casablanca** 1942

— If you're free later this evening...
— I'm never free, sweetie.

> John Gallaudet and Gina Lollobrigida
> **Go Naked in the World** 1961

— Will you dine with me tonight?
— I just met you.
— What about tomorrow night?
— I'll have forgotten you.

> Roland Young and Greta Garbo
> **Two-Faced Woman** 1941

Last night she was banging on my door for
45 minutes — but I wouldn't let her out.

> Dean Martin
> **Kiss Me, Stupid** 1964

Come up again, anytime, Warm, Dark and
Handsome.

> Mae West to Cary Grant
> **She Done Him Wrong** 1933

Why don't you get out of those wet clothes
and into a dry martini?

> Robert Benchley to Ginger Rogers
> **The Major and the Minor** 1942

This may come as a shock to you, but there
are some men who don't end every sentence
with a proposition.

> Doris Day to Rock Hudson
> **Pillow Talk** 1959

# MANHUNT

Five thousand pounds a year and unmarried.
That's the most heartening piece of news
since Waterloo!

> Mary Boland
> **Pride and Prejudice** 1940

Find 'em, fool 'em, and forget 'em.

> Mae West
> **I'm No Angel** 1933

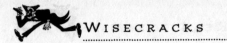

— I could love you body and soul.
— They're available — in that order.

Joan Collins and Bob Hope
**Road to Hong Kong** 1962

The longer they wait, the better they like it.

Marlene Dietrich
**Destry Rides Again** 1939

— You certainly know the way to a man's
heart.
— Funny, too, because I don't know how to
cook.

Libby Taylor and Mae West
**Belle of the Nineties** 1934

You have no idea what a long-legged gal can
do without doing anything.

Claudette Colbert
**The Palm Beach Story** 1942

She's got those eyes that run up and down a
man like a searchlight.

> Dennie Moore
> **The Women** 1939

– Take care of these men.
– Give them all my address.

> John Miljan and Mae West
> **Belle of the Nineties** 1934

A man in the house is worth two in the
street.

> Mae West
> **Belle of the Nineties** 1934

Tell me why it is that every man who seems
attractive these days is either married or
barred on a technicality.

> Celeste Holm
> **Gentleman's Agreement** 1947

He ain't like the other men you done made
history of.

> Louise Beaver to Mae West about Cary Grant
> **She Done Him Wrong** 1933

Six foot four inches of opportunity doesn't
come along every day.

> Thelma Ritter to Doris Day
> **Pillow Talk** 1959

— I hardly know the man.
— Takes only one sip of wine to know if it's a
good bottle.

> Doris Day and Thelma Ritter
> **Pillow Talk** 1959

— Now, look, I hardly know the man.
— Sure, but you'll get over it.

> Jean Arthur and Thomas Mitchell about Cary Grant
> **Only Angels Have Wings** 1939

I look upon him like any other disease. I've had him. It's over. I'm immune to him.

> Doris Day about Rock Hudson
> **Pillow Talk** 1959

I thought he was just a rat, but he was a superrat all along. A superrat in rat's clothing.

> Audrey Hepburn
> **Breakfast at Tiffany's** 1961

He's so low, when they bury him they're gonna have to dig up.

> Audrey Meadows
> **That Touch of Mink** 1962

Looks like Tall, Dark and Legal has stood you up tonight.

> Tyrone Power to Anne Baxter
> **The Razor's Edge** 1946

111

– Don't you think of anything but men?
– Oh yes, dear... schoolboys.

Jeanette MacDonald and Myrna Loy
**Love Me Tonight** 1932

# WOMANHUNT

Why don't we spend one night talking to someone with higher voices than us?

Walter Matthau to Jack Lemmon
**The Odd Couple** 1968

I'd be equally as willing for a dentist to be drilling than to ever let a woman in my life.

Rex Harrison
**My Fair Lady** 1964

– Are you a man of good character where
women are concerned?
– Have you ever met a man of good
character where women are concerned?

> Wilfred Hyde-White and Rex Harrison
> **My Fair Lady** 1964

I'd prefer a new edition of the Spanish
Inquisition than to ever let a woman in my
life.

> Rex Harrison
> **My Fair Lady** 1964

# SEDUCTION

A lot of weather we've been having lately.

> Oliver Hardy chatting up a lady
> **Way Out West** 1937

It's nights like this that drive men like me to women like you for nights like this.

Bob Hope to Hedy Lamarr
**My Favorite Spy** 1951

I'll meet you tonight under the moon. Oh, I can see you now, you and the moon. You wear a necktie so I'll know you.

Groucho Marx to Margaret Dumont
**The Cocoanuts** 1929

Have the florist send some roses to Mrs Upjohn and write 'Emily, I love you' on the back of the bill.

Groucho Marx
**A Day at the Races** 1937

– You smell good. What is it?
– Bug repellent.

Frank Sinatra and Martha Hyer
**Some Came Running** 1958

Excuse me while I brush the crumbs out of
my bed. I'm expecting company.

Groucho Marx
**Duck Soup** 1933

See anything you like?

Barbara Stanwyck to Henry Fonda
**The Lady Eve** 1941

— I wonder if I know what you mean.
— I wonder if you wonder.

Barbara Stanwyck and Fred MacMurray
**Double Indemnity** 1944

The moment I saw you, I had an idea you
had an idea.

Claudette Colbert to John Barrymore
**Midnight** 1939

— What are you thinking of?
— All the years I wasted collecting stamps.

Margaret Dumont and Groucho Marx
**Duck Soup** 1933

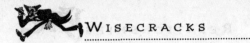

– There's a speed limit in this state, Mr Neff,
45 miles an hour.
– How fast was I going, officer?
– I'd say around 90.

Barbara Stanwyck thinks Fred MacMurray is coming
on too strong
**Double Indemnity** 1944

I'm not to be had for the price of a cocktail –
like a salted peanut.

Bette Davis
**All About Eve** 1950

I don't pop my cork for every man I meet.

Chorus Girls
**Sweet Charity** 1969

I'm hard to get. All you have to do is ask me.

Jean Arthur to Cary Grant
**Only Angels Have Wings** 1939

– You baaad girl.
– You'll find out.

Cary Grant and Mae West
**She Done Him Wrong** 1933

– Don't be so free with your hands.
– Listen, honey, I was only trying to guess your weight.

Jody Gilbert and W.C. Fields
**Never Give a Sucker an Even Break** 1941

– Surely you don't mind my holding your hand?
– It ain't heavy. I can hold it myself.

Cary Grant and Mae West
**She Done Him Wrong** 1933

You have a very hot hand...for an aunt.

Michael Sarrazin to Eleanor Parker
**Eye of the Cat** 1969

It's going to be a long night...and I don't
particularly like the book I started. You know
what I mean?

Eva Marie Saint to Cary Grant
**North by Northwest** 1959

At this time of night, I'm not looking for
needlepoint.

Claudette Colbert to Don Ameche
**Midnight** 1939

I tell you, if I didn't have such a splendid
education, I'd yield to the animal in me.

Charles Ruggles to Jeanette Macdonald
**One Hour With You** 1932

I think if I ever got the bit between your
teeth, I'd have no trouble in handling you at
all.

Joan Fontaine to Cary Grant
**Suspicion** 1941

She was selling hard, but I wasn't buying.

Fred Astaire about Cyd Charisse
**The Band Wagon** 1953


— You mustn't be found in my room. If
necessary, I will scream for help.
— Oh, I don't need any help.

Audrey Dalton and Bob Hope
**Casanova's Big Night** 1954


— I have a complaint.
— Why, what's the matter?
— Do you know who sneaked into my room at
three o'clock this morning?
— Who?
— Nobody, and that's my complaint.

Groucho Marx and Ben Taggart
**Monkey Business** 1931


— Guess I'm taking your time?
— What d'ya s'pose mah time's for?

Cary Grant and Mae West
**She Done Him Wrong** 1933

Go ahead, put Christmas in your eyes and keep your voice low. Tell me about paradise and all the things I'm missing.

Humphrey Bogart to Lizabeth Scott
**Dead Reckoning** 1947

You don't have to act with me, Steve. You don't have to say anything, and you don't have to do anything. Not a thing. Oh, maybe just whistle. You know how to whistle, don't you, Steve? You just put your lips together and...blow.

Lauren Bacall to Humphrey Bogart
**To Have and Have Not** 1945

I've been chased by women before but not while I was awake.

Bob Hope
**The Paleface** 1948

− Hold me closer, closer, closer!
− If I hold you any closer, I'll be in back of
you.

Esther Muir and Groucho Marx
**A Day at the Races** 1937


Is that a gun in your pocket or are you just
glad to see me?

Mae West
**Myra Breckinridge** 1970


I'm afraid you've caught me with more than
my hands up.

Sean Connery
**Diamonds Are Forever** 1971


− Must you flirt?
− I don't have to, but I find it natural.
− Suppress it.

Greta Garbo and Melvyn Douglas
**Ninotchka** 1939

— Why have you brought me here?
— Are you not woman enough to know?

Agnes Ayres and Rudolph Valentino
**The Sheik** 1921

# KISS

— I've never kissed a woman before.
— Before what?

John Beal and Katharine Hepburn
**The Little Minister** 1934

Ah'd love t' kiss yuh, but Ah just washed
mah ha-yer.

Bette Davis
**Cabin in the Cotton** 1932

— You never even tried to kiss me.
— I never could get that close.

Jayne Mansfield and Groucho Marx
**Will Success Spoil Rock Hunter?** 1957

– C'mere. Bruise my lips.
– I think I'll choke you.

Marlene Dietrich and John Lund
**A Foreign Affair** 1948

– I'd rather kiss a tarantula.
– You don't mean that.
– Hey, Joe, bring me a tarantula.

Gene Kelly and Jean Hagen
**Singin' in the Rain** 1952

– I want you to stay away from me.
– No, you don't. Why don't you jump in and get wet all over?

Lana Turner and Clark Gable
**Honky Tonk** 1941

It's even better when you help.

Lauren Bacall to Humphrey Bogart
**To Have and Have Not** 1944

— I got a funny sensation in my toes...like someone was barbecuing them over a slow flame.

— Let's throw another log on the fire.

> Tony Curtis kissing Marilyn Monroe
> **Some Like It Hot** 1959

She had so much bridgework, every time I kissed her I had to pay a toll.

> Lou Costello
> **Abbott and Costello Meet Frankenstein** 1948

— Where did you learn to kiss like that?

— I used to blow a bugle for the Boy Scouts.

> Sally Eilers and Eddie Cantor
> **Strike Me Pink** 1936

William, that was *not* a preacher's kiss.

> Susan Haywood is shocked by her preacher-
> husband's passion
> **I'd Climb The Highest Mountain** 1951

124

– Have there been many?
– I'm afraid so. Quite a few. One night, when I couldn't sleep, I started to count them, you know, like you count sheep jumping a fence. I think I passed out on number 73.

Joan Fontaine and Cary Grant on how many women
he's kissed
**Suspicion** 1941

For the woman, the kiss: for the man, the sword.

Erik Rhodes
**Top Hat** 1935

# SEX

My psychiatrist asked me if I thought sex was dirty and I said it is if you're doing it right.

Woody Allen
**Take the Money and Run** 1969

She uses sex like some people use a fly-swatter.

> Cary Grant about Eva Marie Saint
> **North by Northwest** 1959

Do you think it will ever take the place of night baseball?

> Deborah Kerr to Cary Grant
> **An Affair to Remember** 1957

— It's hard to believe that you haven't had sex for 200 years.
— 204 if you count my marriage.

> Diane Keaton and Woody Allen
> **Sleeper** 1973

The only people who make love all the time are liars.

> Louis Jordan
> **Gigi** 1958

— So I've sown a few wild oats.
— A few? You could qualify for a farm loan.

Rock Hudson and Doris Day
**Pillow Talk** 1959

I can feel the hot blood pounding through
your varicose veins.

Jimmy Durante to Mary Wickes
**The Man Who Came to Dinner** 1941

— Have you got a woman in here?
— If I haven't, I've wasted 30 minutes of
valuable time.

Chico Marx and Groucho Marx
**A Day at the Races** 1937

Do you take travellers' checks?

Tourist Punter to Shirley MacLaine as a streetwalker
in Paris
**Irma La Douce** 1963

127

When it comes to sex, men can't keep from lying and women can't keep from telling the truth.

Kim Novak
**Boys' Night Out** 1962


# LOVE

— Mack, you ever been in love?
— No, I been a bartender all ma life.

Henry Fonda and J. Farrell MacDonald
**My Darling Clementine** 1946


— Have you ever been in love, detective?
— A dame in Washington Heights once got a fox fur out of me.

Clifton Webb and Dana Andrews
**Laura** 1944

— Know anything about love?
— Not me, I'm a married man.

Jane Frazee and Frank Darien
**Hellzapoppin** 1941

You don't know what love means. To you, it's just another four-letter word.

Elizabeth Taylor to Paul Newman
**Cat on a Hot Tin Roof** 1958

Love is something that goes on between a man and a .45 that won't jam.

Alan Ladd
**Appointment With Danger** 1951

Love? Why don't you call it by its real name?

Chester Morris
**Red Headed Woman** 1932

129

Love is a romantic designation for a most
ordinary biological or, shall we say, chemi-
cal process. A lot of nonsense is talked and
written about it.

Greta Garbo
**Ninotchka** 1939

To have to say 'I love you' would break my
teeth.

Anthony Quinn
**Lust for Life** 1956

— I love you.
— What are you trying to do, steal my
gag-line?

Jean Harlow and Clark Gable
**Saratoga** 1937

I love you almost as much as you do.

Walter Matthau to Jack Lemmon
**The Odd Couple** 1968

I love you! It's the old, old story. Boy meets girl, Romeo and Juliet, Minneapolis and St Paul.

Groucho Marx to Margaret Dumont
**A Day at the Races** 1937

I love him... He looks like a giraffe, and I love him.

Barbara Stanwyck about Gary Cooper
**Ball of Fire** 1941

Never fall in love during a total eclipse.

Michael Hordern
**A Funny Thing Happened On the Way to the Forum**
1966

— Do you believe in love at first sight?
— I don't know, but it sure saves time.

George Raft and Mae West
**Night After Night** 1932

— Forget her. There are plenty more fish in
the sea.
— He's not in love with a fish. It's a girl he
loves.

Billy Engle and Stan Laurel
**The Flying Deuces** 1939

— I love you and I want to marry you.
— I love you and I want to marry you.
— That cuts our love scene down quite a bit,
doesn't it?

Joel McCrea and Laraine Day
**Foreign Correspondent** 1940

# MARRIAGE

— I don't suppose you believe in marriage.
— Only as a last resort.

Gertrude Michael and Mae West
**I'm No Angel** 1933

I always felt that you were *above* marriage.

Katharine Hepburn to Fay Bainter
**Woman of the Year** 1942

An outmoded silly convention started by the cavemen and encouraged by the florists and jewelers.

Olivia de Havilland on marriage
**The Strawberry Blonde** 1941

Marriage is forever. It's like cement.

Peter O'Toole
**What's New, Pussycat?** 1965

— You don't marry someone you just met the day before.
— But that's the only way, dear. If you get to know too much about them, you'd never marry them.

Rudy Vallee and Mary Astor
**The Palm Beach Story** 1942

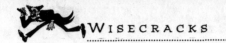

— You're 40, he's 22. Do you have to marry
him?
— As opposed to what?
— Couldn't you just adopt him?

Gene Kelly and Liv Ullmann
**40 Carats** 1973

Make him feel important. If you do that,
you'll have a happy and wonderful
marriage – like two out of every ten couples.

Mildred Natwick to Jane Fonda
**Barefoot in the Park** 1967

Will you marry me? Did he leave you any
money? Answer the second question first.

Groucho Marx to Margaret Dumont
**Duck Soup** 1933

Marry me, Emily, and I'll never look at any
other horse.

Groucho Marx to Margaret Dumont
**A Day at the Races** 1937

I cook. I swallow swords. I mend my own
socks. I never eat garlic or onions. What
more could you ask of a man?

> Vincent Price
> **Laura** 1944

– I'm afraid that after we've been married a
while a beautiful young girl will come along
and you'll forget all about me.
– Don't be silly, I'll write you twice a week.

> Margaret Dumont and Groucho Marx
> **The Big Store** 1941

I wanted to marry her when I first saw the
moonlight shining on the barrel of her
father's shotgun.

> Eddie Albert
> **Oklahoma!** 1956

— Didn't I tell you I was going to get
married?
— Who to?
— Why, a woman, of course. Did you ever
hear of anybody marrying a man?
— Sure.
— Who?
— My sister.

Oliver Hardy and Stan Laurel
**Beau Hunks** 1931


— I'll give you one last chance. Will you
marry me?
— No.
— Let's make it two out of three.

Joan Davis and Eddie Cantor
**Show Business** 1944


— You cannot die an old maid.
— I have no intention to. I shall die a
bachelor.

Lewis Stone and Greta Garbo
**Queen Christina** 1933

– Rather than marry you, I would dive naked into a barrel of rattlesnakes.
– That's final, I take it?

Monty Woolley and Sara Allgood
**Life Begins at Eight Thirty** 1942

– You're a guy. Why should a guy want to marry a guy?
– Security.

Tony Curtis to Jack Lemmon
**Some Like It Hot** 1959

– I'm gonna level with you. We can't get married at all...I'm a man.
– Well, nobody's perfect.

Jack Lemmon in drag and Joe E. Brown
**Some Like It Hot** 1959

I do. And may heaven have mercy on my soul.

William Powell marrying Jean Arthur
**The Ex-Mrs Bradford** 1936

— What would you like to see on your honeymoon?

— Lots and lots of lovely ceilings.

George Peppard and Elizabeth Ashley
**The Carpetbaggers** 1964

We went to Mexico on our honeymoon.
Spent the entire two weeks in bed. I had
dysentery.

Woody Allen
**Play It Again, Sam** 1972

Here comes that exotic star, Olga Mara and
her new husband, the Baron de la May de la
Toulon. They've been married two months
already but are still as happy as ever.

Madge Blake
**Singin' in the Rain** 1952

Been married 38 years myself, and I don't regret one day of it. The one day of it I don't regret was August 2nd 1936. She was off visiting her ailing mother at the time.

Eddie Mayehoff
**How to Murder Your Wife** 1964

– You never met my wife, did you?
– Yes, I never did.

Oliver Hardy and Stan Laurel
**Helpmates** 1932

No matter who you get married to, you wake up married to somebody else.

Marlon Brando
**Guys and Dolls** 1955

All wives start out as Juliets and end up as Lady Macbeths.

William Holden
**The Country Girl** 1954

Life with Mary was like being in a phone booth with an open umbrella. No matter which way you turned, you got it in the eye.

Barry Nelson
**Mary, Mary** 1963

– Do you have to ask your wife everything?
– Well, if I didn't ask her, I wouldn't know what she wanted me to do.

Oliver Hardy and Stan Laurel
**Sons of the Desert** 1933

– Aren't you forgetting that you're married?
– I'm doing my best.

Dick Foran and Mae West
**My Little Chickadee** 1940

# CHEATING

Pardon me, but your husband is showing.

Glenn Ford to Rita Hayworth
**Gilda** 1946

I've known and respected your husband for
years, and what's good enough for him is
good enough for me.

> Groucho Marx to Thelma Todd
> **Monkey Business** 1931

We promise to be faithful...until the night is
through.

> Maurice Chevalier
> **A Bedtime Story** 1933

– I know Manny Davis.
– Everyone knows Manny Davis – except Mrs
Manny Davis.

> Tony Curtis and Burt Lancaster
> **Sweet Smell of Success** 1957

You know, the first man that can think up a good explanation how he can be in love with his wife *and* another woman is gonna win that prize they're always giving out in Sweden.

Mary Cecil
**The Women** 1939

You mustn't think too harshly of my secretaries. They were very kind and understanding when I came to the office after a hard day at home.

Claude Rains
**Mr Skeffington** 1944

– Those affairs meant nothing. After all, a man must live.
– Why?

Ben Lyon and Gloria Swanson
**Indiscreet** 1931

142

The only thing I ever ask any woman is,
What time is your husband coming home?

>Paul Newman to Patricia Neal
>**Hud** 1963

What is the surest way to keep a husband
home? Break both his legs.

>Title Card (Laurel and Hardy)
>**Should Married Men Go Home** 1928

– She's married now – got a husband.
– Oh yeah? Whose husband she got?

>William Powell and Myrna Loy
>**Love Crazy** 1941

Say, can you beat him? He almost stood me
up for his wife.

>Joan Crawford
>**The Women** 1939

When you're in love with a married man,
you shouldn't wear mascara.

> Shirley Maclaine
> **The Apartment** 1960

# DIVORCE

Why don't you get a divorce and settle
down?

> Oscar Levant to Joan Crawford
> **Humoresque** 1947

In our family we don't divorce our men. We
bury them.

> Ruth Gordon
> **Lord Love a Duck** 1966

I swear, if you existed, I'd divorce you.

> Elizabeth Taylor to Richard Burton
> **Who's Afraid of Virginia Woolf?** 1966

— Why did you two ever get married?
— Oh, I don't know. It was raining, and we were in Pittsburgh.

Barbara Stanwyck and Helen Broderick
**The Bride Walks Out** 1936

I thought it was for life, but the old judge gave me a full pardon.

Katharine Hepburn about her marriage to Cary Grant
**The Philadelphia Story** 1940

You got an old-fashioned idea that a divorce is something that lasts forever, till death do us part.

Cary Grant to Rosalind Russell
**His Girl Friday** 1940

# CHILDREN

– We're going to have a baby. That's my
Christmas present to you.
– All I needed was a tie.

> Janet Margolin and Woody Allen
> **Take the Money and Run** 1969

– Don't you like children?
– No. They always seem to be so wise.

> Claude Rains and Bette Davis
> **Mr Skeffington** 1944

– Do you like children?
– I do if they're properly cooked.

> Alison Skipworth and W.C. Fields
> **Tillie and Gus** 1933

Alligators have the right idea. They eat their
young.

> Eve Arden
> **Mildred Pierce** 1945

146

I bet your father spent the first year of your
life throwing rocks at the stork.

Groucho Marx
**At the Circus** 1939

From the looks of those ears, she's gonna fly
before she walks.

Lawrence Tierney looking at a baby photo
**The Devil Thumbs a Ride** 1947

— He's getting more like his father each day.
— He sure is. This morning I found him
playing with the corkscrew.

Myrna Loy and Louise Beavers
**Shadow of the Thin Man** 1941

You kids are disgusting, skulking around
here all day, reeking of popcorn and
lollipops.

W.C. Fields
**You Can't Cheat an Honest Man** 1939

— You can't throw your own daughter over-
board.
— Why not? Let the sharks protect themselves.

Ben Blue and W.C. Fields
**The Big Broadcast of 1938** 1938

Twins are so practical. It's always nice to
have a spare.

Billie Burke
**Hi Diddle Diddle** 1943

# ADVICE

— You're getting to be a big boy now, son,
and there comes a time when we must dis-
cuss some of the mysteries of life.
— Yes, father, what do you wish to know?

Sylvester the Cat and Junior
**Who's Kitten Who?** 1952

148

Never apologize and never explain. It's a
sign of weakness.

John Wayne
**She Wore a Yellow Ribbon** 1949

Myrtle Mae, you have a lot to learn...and I
hope you never learn it.

Josephine Hull
**Harvey** 1950

Take care of your body, Maisie, because it's
all you've got.

Dorothy Kent
**More Than a Secretary** 1936

I always say, keep a diary and some day it'll
keep you.

Mae West
**Every Day's a Holiday** 1937

You've buttered your bread, now sleep in it.

Porky Pig to the bear
**Porky's Bear Facts** 1941

# FRIENDS AND ENEMIES

Don't worry, I may be rancid butter, but I'm on your side of the bread.

Gene Kelly to Donna Anderson
**Inherit the Wind** 1960

You know, Speedy, I like your pussycat friend. He's nice and stupid.

Slowpoke Rodriguez to Speedy Gonzales about
Sylvester
**Mexican Borders** 1962

He hasn't an enemy in the world. Only his friends hate him.

Gene Kelly about Fredric March
**Inherit the Wind** 1960

# HUMAN NATURE

# CHARACTER

– I have heard so much about you.
– Yeah, but you can't prove it.

> Gilbert Roland and Mae West
> **She Done Him Wrong** 1933

It's not a pretty face, I grant you, but underneath its flabby exterior is an enormous lack of character.

> Oscar Levant
> **An American in Paris** 1951

I've often speculated on why you don't return to America. Did you abscond with the church funds? Did you run off with a Senator's wife? I'd like to think you killed a man. It's the romantic in me.

> Claude Rains to Humphrey Bogart
> **Casablanca** 1942

152

Kitteridge is no great tower of strength. He's just a tower.

> Cary Grant about John Howard
> **The Philadelphia Story** 1940

She has a shoulder that would make dry ice feel like a bed-warmer.

> Melvyn Douglas about Rosalind Russell
> **This Thing Called Love** 1941

I grow on people – like moss.

> Mary Astor
> **The Palm Beach Story** 1942

I'm not kind, I'm vicious. It's the secret of my charm.

> Clifton Webb
> **Laura** 1944

What can a Saxon hedge robber know of charm?

> Olivia de Havilland to Errol Flynn
> **The Adventures of Robin Hood** 1938

Bridge at three...dinner at eight. And after dinner, bridge. Rather an amusing day, eh, Flamand?

C. Aubrey Smith
**Love Me Tonight** 1932

— Are you busy?
— I'm about as busy as a pickpocket in a nudist colony.

Irving Bacon and W.C. Fields
**Six of a Kind** 1934

It was the busiest part of the day, damn it, I was tying my cravat.

Leslie Howard
**The Scarlet Pimpernel** 1934

I haven't time. I'm much too busy seeing that you don't lose any of the money I married you for.

William Powell to Myrna Loy
**The Thin Man** 1934

— Did you say you can tear the telephone
book in half?
— Yessir.
— Wait a minute, wait a minute! You're
tearing one page at a time.
— I ain't in a hurry.

> Eddie Cantor and Harry Einstein
> **Strike Me Pink** 1936

Funny, the moment you get someone else
worrying, you stop worrying yourself.

> Spencer Tracy
> **Father of the Bride** 1950

Failure is the only thing I've ever been a
success at.

> Bob Hope
> **Here Come the Girls** 1957

— Why did you have to go on?
— Too many people told me to stop.

> Lauren Bacall and Humphrey Bogart
> **The Big Sleep** 1946

— Are you sure you have everything, Otis?
— I've never had any complaints yet.

Margaret Dumont asking Groucho Marx about some
luggage
**A Night at the Opera** 1935


He was a poet, a scholar and a mighty
warrior. He was also the most shameless
exhibitionist since Barnum and Bailey.

Arthur Kennedy about Peter O'Toole
**Lawrence of Arabia** 1962


I wish someone would tell you what I really
think of you.

Claudette Colbert to Gary Cooper
**Bluebeard's Eighth Wife** 1938

# INTELLIGENCE

— You know, Ollie, I was just thinking.
— About what?
— Nothing. I was just thinking.

Oliver Hardy and Stan Laurel
**Jitterbugs** 1943

This is Mr Englund, the brains of the
organization. That'll give you some idea of
the organization.

Groucho Marx
**Room Service** 1938

Barovelli, you've got the brain of a four-
year-old boy and I bet he was glad to get rid
of it.

Groucho Marx
**Horse Feathers** 1932

Chicolini here may talk like an idiot and look like an idiot. But don't let that fool you. He really is an idiot.

> Groucho Marx
> **Duck Soup** 1933

The kid's about as sharp as a pound of wet liver.

> Foghorn Leghorn to Henery Hawk
> **Hen House Henery** 1949

If a gnat dived into your pool of knowledge, it would break its neck.

> Cary Grant to Ginger Rogers
> **Once Upon a Honeymoon** 1942

What do you think I am, dumb or something? Why, I make more money than Calvin Coolidge – put together!

> Jean Hagen
> **Singin' in the Rain** 1952

I can be smart when it's important, but most
men don't like it.

Marilyn Monroe
**Gentlemen Prefer Blondes** 1953

I don't know a lot about anything, but I
know a little about practically everything.

Vincent Price
**Laura** 1944

His brain has not only been washed. It has
been dry-cleaned.

Joe Adams
**The Manchurian Candidate** 1962

— I thought that was rather clever of me.
— Yes, I thought you thought so.

William Powell and Myrna Loy
**Libeled Lady** 1936

We're intellectual opposites. I'm intellectual
and you're opposite.

Mae West
**Goin' to Town** 1935

– How stupid can you get?
– How stupid do you want me?

Bud Abbott and Lou Costello
**Abbott and Costello Meet Frankenstein** 1948

– Don't you want to be smart?
– No, I want to be like you.

W.C. Fields and Gloria Jean
**Never Give a Sucker an Even Break** 1941

– I'm nobody's fool.
– An orphan, huh?

Jack Oakie and Gracie Allen
**Big Broadcast of 1936** 1936

— Any man's a fool who's certain about
anything.
— Are you sure, sir?
— Positive.

Hugh Herbert and Eric Blore
**To Beat the Band** 1935

Clear? Why, a four-year-old child could
understand this report. Run out and get me a
four-year-old child. I can't make head nor
tail out of it.

Groucho Marx
**Duck Soup** 1933

— I've changed my mind.
— Yeah, does it work any better?

Edward Arnold and Mae West
**I'm No Angel** 1933

# SUCKERS

There's as fine a specimen of the *sucker sapiens* as I've ever seen.

Charles Coburn about Henry Fonda
**The Lady Eve** 1941

Never give a sucker an even break.

W.C. Fields
**Poppy** 1936

Some people take and some people get took.

Shirley Maclaine
**The Apartment** 1960

You've been taken to the cleaners and you don't even know your pants are off.

Myrna Loy to Cary Grant
**Mr Blandings Build His Dream House** 1948

162

That's the first mistake we've made since
that guy sold us the Brooklyn Bridge.

> Stan Laurel
> **Way Out West** 1937

# MADNESS

Insanity runs in my family. It practically
gallops.

> Cary Grant
> **Arsenic and Old Lace** 1944

I'm going crazy. I'm standing here solidly on
my own two hands, and going crazy.

> Katharine Hepburn
> **The Philadelphia Story** 1940

All you need to start an asylum is an empty
room and the right kind of people.

> Eugene Pallette
> **My Man Godfrey** 1936

Women make the best psychoanalysts till they fall in love. After that, they make the best patients.

Michael Chekhov to Ingrid Bergman
**Spellbound** 1945

This is Miss Hambridge, our new school teacher. She's between nervous breakdowns.

Margaret Hamilton
**The Moon's Our Home** 1936

— I'm sure there's nothing wrong with me.
— I'm sure you'll think differently after you leave this office.

Merle Oberon and pyschoanalyst Alan Mowbray
**That Uncertain Feeling** 1941

He told me I had a dual personality. Then he lays an 82 dollar tab on me, so I give him 41 bucks and say, 'Get the other 41 bucks from the other guy.'

Jerry Lewis
**The Nutty Professor** 1963

– There are worse things than chastity, Mr
Shannon.
– Yes, lunacy and death.

Deborah Kerr and Richard Burton
**The Night of the Iguana** 1964

# CLASS

Do you mean to stand there and tell me I
ain't got class?

Vivian Blaine
**Cover Girl** 1945

You look like you got class... yessir. With a
capital K!

Roscoe Karns to Claudette Colbert
**It Happened One Night** 1934

– Speaking of horses...you've got a touch of
class but I don't know how far you can go.
– A lot depends on who's in the saddle.

> Humphrey Bogart and Lauren Bacall
> **The Big Sleep** 1946

So, you want to learn class. Lesson number
one: an Etruscan vase is not a flower pot.

> David Brian to Joan Crawford
> **The Damned Don't Cry** 1950

# MANNERS

– Let's begin with posture. A lady always
enters a room erect.
– Lots of my friends exit horizontally.

> Ann Morriss and Rosalind Russell
> **The Women** 1939

I got two rules I always stick to when I'm out
visitin'. Keep away from couches, and stay on
your feet.

Jean Harlow
**Hold Your Man** 1933

Agatha might commit a sin, but she'd never
commit a faux pas.

Lowell Sherman
**Bachelor Apartment** 1931

It's Mr Barker! Get out the good cup and
saucer and give it a wipe.

Dorothy McGuire
**A Tree Grows in Brooklyn** 1945

Bad table manners, my dear Gigi, have
broken up more households than infidelity.

Isabel Jeans to Leslie Caron
**Gigi** 1958

Don't say 'stinks', darling. If absolutely
necessary, 'smells', but only if absolutely
necessary.

> Mary Nash to Virginia Weidler
> **The Philadelphia Story** 1940

Don't flop into the chair. Insinuate yourself.

> Isabel Jeans to Leslie Caron
> **Gigi** 1958

Chivalry is not only dead. It's decomposed.

> Rudy Vallee
> **The Palm Beach Story** 1942

I don't mind if you don't like my manners. I
don't like 'em myself. They're pretty bad. I
grieve over them long winter evenings.

> Humphrey Bogart
> **The Big Sleep** 1946

I don't dally much with riff-raff these days,
and he's a pretty raffy kind of riff.

> Bob Hope about Bing Crosby
> **The Road to Morocco** 1942

# VANITY

– You're wonderful.
– Of course. Didn't you know?

> Spencer Tracy and Katharine Hepburn
> **Woman of the Year** 1942

He fell in love with himself the first time he
looked in the mirror and he's been faithful
ever since.

> Mitzi Gaynor about Gene Kelly
> **Les Girls** 1957

I'm not worth it. But if I'm not, who is?

> Bob Hope
> **The Great Lover** 1949

– You don't need mystery. You've got
something more alluring.
– What?
– Me.

William Powell and Myrna Loy
**After the Thin Man** 1936

In my case, self-absorption is completely
justified. I have never discovered any other
subject quite so worthy of my attention.

Clifton Webb
**Laura** 1944

No, you're wrong, girls, you're wrong! In the
first place, Gary Cooper is much taller than I
am.

Groucho Marx
**Monkey Business** 1931

Oh, I wish I was a girl so I could fight over
me.

Bob Hope
**Here Come the Girls** 1953

You know, I'm so smart sometimes, it almost frightens me.

Bugs Bunny
**Jack Wabbit and the Beanstalk** 1943

# BELIEFS

My religion? My dear, I'm a millionaire. That's my religion.

Robert Morley
**Major Barbara** 1941

I don't go to church. Kneeling bags my nylons.

Jan Sterling
**Ace in the Hole** 1951

If there's one place the church should leave alone, it's a man's soul.

William Powell
**Life With Father** 1947

Don't give me any of that sister, come to
salvation look. I'm not buying any. I know
the routine. It starts out with a prayer, and
ends up with the bible in one hand and me
in the other.

> Joan Crawford to Ian Hunter
> **Strange Cargo** 1940

I like my convictions undiluted, same as I do
my bourbon.

> George Brent
> **Jezebel** 1938

I know there's no such thing as Dracula. You
know there's no such thing as Dracula. But
does Dracula know it?

> Lou Costello
> **Abbott and Costello Meet Frankenstein** 1948

In a world where carpenters get resurrected,
anything is possible.

> Peter O'Toole
> **The Lion in Winter** 1968

172

# TRUTH AND LIES

There are three sides to every story: yours, his and the truth.

Madge Kennedy
**The Marrying Kind** 1952

That's our story, and we're stuck with it.

Stan Laurel
**Them Thar Hills** 1934

We didn't exactly believe your story, Miss O'Shaughnessy. We believed your 200 dollars.

Humphrey Bogart to Mary Astor
**The Maltese Falcon** 1941

Isn't it monstrous the way people go about saying things behind people's backs that are absolutely and entirely true?

George Sanders
**The Picture of Dorian Gray** 1945

– Tell me lies.
– I have waited for you, Johnny.

> Sterling Hayden and Joan Crawford
> **Johnny Guitar** 1954

People will believe any lie if it is fantastic enough.

> Leo Genn
> **Quo Vadis** 1951

There is no sincerity like a woman telling a lie.

> Cecil Parker
> **Indiscreet** 1958

Those ain't lies. Those are campaign promises.

> William Demarest
> **Hail the Conquering Hero** 1944

I'm honest because, with you, I think it's the best way to get results.

Cary Grant to Joan Fontaine
**Suspicion** 1941

— If only I could trust you.
— Hundreds have.

Cary Grant and Mae West
**She Done Him Wrong** 1933

You're as phony to me as an opera soprano.

William Holden to Grace Kelly
**The Country Girl** 1954

She's a phony, *but* she's a real phony.

Martin Balsam about Audrey Hepburn
**Breakfast at Tiffany's** 1961

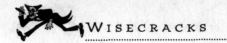

# GOOD AND BAD

– Are you in town for good?
– I expect to be here, but not for good.

> Sam McDaniel and Mae West
> **Belle of the Nineties** 1934

When I'm good, I'm very, very good, but when I'm bad, I'm better.

> Mae West
> **I'm No Angel** 1933

– Who'd want me after what I've done?
– Listen, when women go wrong, men go right after them.

> Rochelle Hudson and Mae West
> **She Done Him Wrong** 1933

A good influence is the worst influence of all.

> George Sanders
> **The Picture of Dorian Gray** 1945

– Have you no morals?
– No, I can't afford 'em.

Rex Harrison and Stanley Holloway
**My Fair Lady** 1964

# BRAVERY AND COWARDICE

I won't need that spear. It's only a *young* lion.

Victor Mature
**Samson and Delilah** 1949

Every man I meet wants to protect me. I can't figure out from what.

Mae West
**My Little Chickadee** 1940

— I whipped out my revolver...
— Revolvers weren't invented 35 years ago.
— I know that, but the Indians didn't know it.

> Fred Kohler and W.C. Fields
> **Mississippi** 1935


— I'm a hero. I was shot twice in *The Tribune*.
— I read where you were shot five times in
the tabloids.
— It's not true. He didn't come anywhere
near my tabloids.

> William Powell and Myrna Loy
> **The Thin Man** 1934


Ah, running off to war like a coward!

> Shrewish Wife to Henpecked Husband
> **I Married a Witch** 1942


— I've never heard my courage questioned.
— I never heard your courage mentioned.

> Bob Hope and Lucille Ball
> **Sorrowful Jones** 1949

Brave men run in my family.

Bob Hope
**The Paleface** 1948

I couldn't save a clam from a bowl of chowder.

Bob Hope
**The Paleface** 1948

I get goose pimples. Even my goose pimples get goose pimples.

Bob Hope
**The Cat and the Canary** 1939

– What are you, man or mouse?
– I'm not a mouse and I'm not a man. I'm a dentist.

Bob Hope's conscience in voice-over and Bob Hope
**The Paleface** 1948

He's got no more nerve than a bum tooth.

Foghorn Leghorn about Henery Hawk
**Henhouse Henery** 1949

— Is it safe?
— Safest thing in the world...would you mind paying me now?

Nestor Paiva as a patient and Bob Hope as a dentist
**The Paleface** 1948

They're not going to torture me. It hurts.

Bob Hope
**Road to Bali** 1952

Of course it hurts. The trick is not *showing* that it hurts.

Peter O'Toole
**Lawrence of Arabia** 1962

– Would you rather die like a hero or live like a rat?
– Get the cheese ready.

> Abbott and Costello
> **Abbott and Costello Meet Frankenstein** 1948

– Don't these big empty houses scare you?
– Not me, I was in vaudeville.

> Nydia Westman and Bob Hope
> **The Cat and the Canary** 1939

– Are you afraid to die, Spartacus?
– No more than I was to be born.

> Tony Curtis and Kirk Douglas
> **Spartacus** 1960

# FUN

Fun? Getting a clear picture on Channel 2 is not my idea of whoopee.

> Walter Matthau to Jack Lemmon
> **The Odd Couple** 1968

181

The only fun I get is feeding the goldfish,
and they only eat once a day.

Bette Davis
**Bordertown** 1935

According to you, everything I like to do is
either illegal, immoral or fattening.

W.C. Fields to Alison Skipworth
**Six of a Kind** 1934

Let's do things we'll live to regret!

Maurice Chevalier
**A Bedtime Story** 1933

– I've never bought things for a girl before –
I mean, in any such quantities.
– You've been denying yourself, monsieur,
one of *the* basic pleasures in life.

Rudy Vallee and Saleswoman
**The Palm Beach Story** 1942

The joy of giving is indeed a pleasure –
especially when you get rid of something you
don't want.

Barry Fitzgerald
**Going My Way** 1944

Let joy be unconfined. Let there be dancing
in the streets, drinking in the saloons and
necking in the park.

Groucho Marx
**A Night at the Opera** 1935

# HAPPINESS

I want you to find happiness and stop having
fun.

Marilyn Monroe to Jane Russell
**Gentlemen Prefer Blondes** 1953

I was never so happy since I kissed my
mother-in-law with a cigar in my mouth.

Bert Lahr
**Josette** 1938

He's much too happy for Sunday, if you ask
me.

Elizabeth Risdon about Melvyn Douglas
**Theodora Goes Wild** 1936

Don't look for happiness. It'll only make you
miserable.

Beatrice Arthur
**Lovers and Other Strangers** 1970

There's all kinds of happiness. This is the
happiness that everyone isn't too happy
about.

Paul Ford
**Never Too Late** 1965

184

# LUCK

– When I look in my crystal ball, do you
know what I see?
– Goldfish?

> Edgar Bergen and Charlie McCarthy
> **Stage Door Canteen** 1943

Let me just pull something out of the hat
here and see if it hops.

> Alan Hewitt
> **Days of Wine and Roses** 1962

I always get the fuzzy end of the lollipop.

> Marilyn Monroe
> **Some Like It Hot** 1959

Well, you look like the kind of angel I'd get.
Sort of fallen angel are you?

> James Stewart to Henry Travers
> **It's a Wonderful Life** 1946

Pull up a coffin and lie down with the rest of us.

Ned Sparks
**Gold Diggers of 1933** 1933

# MEMORY

– I'll never forget you.
– No one ever does.

Kent Taylor and Mae West
**I'm No Angel** 1933

I remember every detail. The Germans wore gray. You wore blue.

Humphrey Bogart to Ingrid Bergman
**Casablanca** 1942

– How many men have you forgotten?
– As many women as you've remembered.

Sterling Hayden and Joan Crawford
**Johnny Guitar** 1954

Snookums, you mean you've forgotten! Those June nights on the Riviera when we sat beneath those shimmering skies, moonlight bathing in the Mediterranean. We were young, gay, reckless! That night I drank champagne from your slipper. Two quarts. It would have been more but you were wearing inner soles.

Groucho Marx to Margaret Dumont
**At the Circus** 1939

— It seems to me we've met before...perhaps in your dreams.
— You wouldn't be seen in those kinds of places.

Dorothy Lamour and Bob Hope
**Road to Utopia** 1945

If I ever forgot myself with that girl, I'd remember it.

Fred Astaire about Ginger Rogers
**Top Hat** 1935

187

# REGRETS

I hope you'll never regret what promises to be a disgustingly earthy relationship.

> Clifton Webb to Gene Tierney
> **Laura** 1944

He'll regret it to his dying day – if ever he lives that long.

> Victor McLaglen about John Wayne
> **The Quiet Man** 1952

As you grow older, you'll find that the only things you regret are the things you didn't do.

> Zachary Scott
> **Mildred Pierce** 1945

The only things one never regrets are one's mistakes.

> George Sanders
> **The Picture of Dorian Gray** 1945

Blessed are those who expect nothing, for
they shall not be disappointed.

Edmund Gwenn
**The Trouble With Harry** 1955

# WORK

I run a couple of newspapers. What do you
do?

Orson Welles
**Citizen Kane** 1941

I loaf – but in a decorative and highly
charming manner.

Zachary Scott
**Possessed** 1947

– I have a half interest in a little farm. I
breed horses.
– What's the matter, they can't do it alone?

Omar Sharif and Barbra Streisand
**Funny Girl** 1968

189

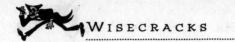

— I got a job at the striptease. I help the girls
dress and undress.
— Nice job.
— Twenty francs a week.
— Not very much.
— It's all I can afford.

> Woody Allen and Peter O'Toole
> **What's New Pussycat?** 1965

I wanted to be a detective. It only took
brains, courage and a gun – and I had the
gun.

> Bob Hope
> **My Favorite Brunette** 1947

Diamonds is my career.

> Mae West
> **She Done Him Wrong** 1933

Modeling is nothing more than organized
walking.

> Model Agent to Jane Fonda
> **Fun With Dick and Jane** 1977

— I was reading a book the other day... The guy said that machinery is going to take the place of *every* profession.
— Oh, my dear, that's something *you* need never worry about.

Jean Harlow and Marie Dressler
**Dinner at Eight** 1933

Michelangelo did his best work on his back.

Van Heflin
**Johnny Eager** 1941

It will be a pleasure serving under you.

Mie Hama to Sean Connery
**You Only Live Twice** 1967

Find someone to type this.

Charles Coburn to secretary, Marilyn Monroe
**Monkey Business** 1952

191

— Aren't you here early?
— Oh, yes, Mr Oxley's been complaining
about my punctuation, so I'm careful to get
here before nine.

> Cary Grant and Marilyn Monroe
> **Monkey Business** 1952

Every day, up at the crack of noon.

> Lucille Ball
> **Mame** 1974

— May I ask what your profession is?
— Certainly, I am a genius.

> Clifton Webb to Maureen O'Hara
> **Sitting Pretty** 1948

I figure I'm in one business that really helps
people. 'Course, we don't help you much
while you're alive but afterward, that's what
counts.

> Ralph Bellamy as an insurance man
> **His Girl Friday** 1940

My father occupied the Chair of Applied
Electricity at the State Prison.

> W.C. Fields
> **The Big Broadcast of 1938** 1938

— I'm a contact man. I keep contact between
Matushek & Co. and the customers — on a
bicycle.
— You mean an errand boy.
— Doctor, did I call you a pill-pedlar?

> James Stewart and Edwin Maxwell
> **The Shop Around the Corner** 1940

Good gardeners are so hard to come by. I
think no woman really had any luck with
gardeners since Lady Chatterley.

> Rosemary Murphy
> **Any Wednesday** 1966

Learn some sort of trade, so at least we'll
know what sort of work you're out of.

> Milton Berle
> **New Faces of 1937** 1937

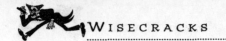

As long as they've got sidewalks, you've got a job.

> Joan Blondell
> **Footlight Parade** 1933

# RICH AND POOR

Here I am, 35, and I ain't even got a good watch.

> Gregory Peck
> **The Gunfighter** 1950

Money talks, they say. All it ever said to me was 'Goodbye'.

> Cary Grant
> **None But the Lonely Heart** 1944

I worked my way up from nothing to a state of extreme poverty.

> Groucho Marx
> **Monkey Business** 1931

Three years ago I came to Florida without a nickel in my pocket. Now I have a nickel in my pocket.

Groucho Marx
**The Cocoanuts** 1939

Remember, you guys, your salaries are paid by the tax payers, and I may be one some day.

Bob Hope to some government officials
**My Favorite Spy** 1953

We had some money put aside for a rainy day, but we didn't know it was going to get this wet.

Jane Connell
**Mame** 1974

– Who's at the door?...It's Fay!
– Who d'ya think it was, the wolf?
– If it was, we'd eat it.

Aline MacMahon, Ginger Rogers and Joan Blondell
**Gold Diggers of 1933** 1933

I've been poor and I've been rich and believe me, rich is better.

Gloria Grahame
**The Big Heat** 1953

Money isn't everything. It can't buy poverty.

Frank Sinatra
**The Joker is Wild** 1957

If the rich could get others to die for them, we, the poor, would make a nice living.

Peasant
**Fiddler on the Roof** 1971

I wasn't always rich. There was a time when I didn't know where my next husband was coming from.

Mae West
**She Done Him Wrong** 1933

A man being rich is like a girl being pretty.
You might not marry a girl just because she's
pretty but, my goodness, doesn't it help?

Marilyn Monroe
**Gentlemen Prefer Blondes** 1953

— Do you expect me to believe that you don't
want to marry my son for his money?
— It's true... I want to marry him for *your*
money.

Marilyn Monroe and Tommy Noonan
**Gentlemen Prefer Blondes** 1953

— Do you play the market?
— No, the ukulele.

Tony Curtis and Marilyn Monroe
**Some Like It Hot** 1959

— Here, boy, take these bags, run up to my
room, and here's a dime for your trouble.
— Oh no, no, no, this is is Mr Whitmore, our
business manager.
— I'm terribly sorry, here's a quarter.

> Groucho Marx and Margaret Dumont
> **A Day at the Races** 1937

— Why should you carry other people's bags?
That's social injustice.
— That depends on the tip.

> Greta Garbo as a communist and a Station Porter
> **Ninotchka** 1939

— Don't make a move. This is a stick-up. Your
money or your life!...Look, bud, I said, your
money or your life!
— I'm thinking it over.

> Mugger and Jack Benny
> **Hollywood Canteen** 1944

# LAW AND ORDER

# MURDER

Mother – what is the phrase? – she isn't
quite herself today.

Anthony Perkins
**Psycho** 1960

Very stupid to kill the only servant in the
house. Now we don't even know where to
find the marmalade.

Judith Anderson
**And Then There Were None** 1945

My boyfriend stabbed himself on a knife I
was holding.

Iris Adrian
**Flamingo Road** 1949

This picture is dedicated to all the beautiful
women of the world who have shot their
husbands full of holes out of pique.

Prologue
**Roxie Hart** 1942

- Where is your husband?
- Why, he's dead.
- I'll bet he's just using that as an excuse.
- I was with him to the very end.
- Huh. No wonder he passed away.
- I held him in my arms and kissed him.
- Oh, I see. Then it was murder.

> Groucho Marx and Margaret Dumont
> **Duck Soup** 1933

Was it murder...or something serious?

> Dick Powell
> **Murder, My Sweet** 1944

I don't like violence, Tom. I'm a business-
man. Murder's a big expense.

> Al Lettieri
> **The Godfather** 1972

Golly, Mr Wabbit, I hope I didn't hurt ya too
much when I killed ya.

> Elmer Fudd to Bugs Bunny
> **Duck! Rabbit, Duck!** 1953

# CRIME

Oh, if only I could steal enough to be an honest man.

Peter Sellers
**After the Fox** 1966

Big Jim was an inspiration to me. When I was a kid, he caught me stealing hubcaps off his car, and he said, 'Kid, don't steal the hubcabs, steal the car'.

Peter Falk
**Robin and the Seven Hoods** 1964

– What could have been the motive of the guys who stole the painting?
– I got it!  Robbery.

Groucho Marx and Chico Marx
**Animal Crackers** 1930

Following in your father's fingerprints, huh?

Bob Hope to an ace safe-cracker
**Road to Utopia** 1945

They tell me he was so crooked that when he
died they had to *screw* him into the ground.

Bob Hope
**The Cat and the Canary** 1939

Even your smile is crooked.

Jean Harlow to Clark Gable
**Hold Your Man** 1933

– Is everybody in this world corrupt?
– I don't know everybody.

Horst Buchholz and Leon Askin
**One, Two, Three** 1961

– Supposing I wasn't a convict. Supposing I
was sailing through on my yacht, or a guy
selling brushes...
– Yeah, and suppose I was Snow White.

Clark Gable and Joan Crawford
**Strange Cargo** 1940

Bigamy; passing as the Prince of Wales; eating spaghetti in public; using hard words in a speakeasy; trumping partner's ace; spitting in the Gulf Stream; jumping board bill in 17 lunatic asylums; failing to pay instalments on a strait-jacket; possessing a skunk; revealing the facts of life to an Indian.

List of accusations on Wanted Poster of W.C. Fields
**The Golf Specialist** 1930


Dammit, why is everything we're good at illegal?

Robert Redford to Paul Newman
**Butch Cassidy and the Sundance Kid** 1969


Major Strasser has been shot. Round up the usual suspects.

Claude Rains
**Casablanca** 1942

Experience has taught me to never trust a policeman. Just when you think one's all right, he turns legit.

Sam Jaffe
**The Asphalt Jungle** 1950

– Are those handcuffs absolutely necessary? You know, I wasn't born with them.
– A lot of men would have been safer if you had.
– I don't know. Hands ain't everything.

Mae West and Cary Grant
**She Done Him Wrong** 1933

# LAW

– Do you think we should send for a lawyer?
– Certainly not. We're in enough trouble.

Bert Wheeler and Robert Woolsey
**Cockeyed Cavaliers** 1934

What do you got instead of a conscience?
Don't answer. I know: a lawyer.

> Kirk Douglas
> **Detective Story** 1951

— You're awfully shy for a lawyer.
— You bet I'm shy. I'm a shyster lawyer.

> Thelma Todd and Groucho Marx
> **Monkey Business** 1931

Oh, Judge, I never swear.

> Jane Russell
> **Gentlemen Prefer Blondes** 1953

— Are you trying to show contempt for this court?
— No, I'm trying my best to hide it.

> Addison Roberts and Mae West
> **My Little Chickadee** 1940

We find the defendants *incredibly* guilty.

> Jury about Gene Wilder and Zero Mostel
> **The Producers** 1967

– There's a lot to be said for prison.
– You always know where you are when you get up in the morning.

Peter Ustinov and Aldo Ray
**We're No Angels** 1955

# WAR AND PEACE

– What's war?
– Trading real estate for men.

Martin Miller and Forrest Tucker
**The Sands of Iwo Jima** 1949

Well, that's war for you – always hard on women. Either they take your men away and never send them back at all or they send them back unexpectedly just to embarrass you.

Elizabeth Patterson
**Hail the Conquering Hero** 1944

Mr President, I'm not saying we wouldn't get our hair mussed, but I do say not more than ten or twenty million killed tops, depending on the breaks.

George C. Scott to Peter Sellers
**Dr Strangelove, Or How I Learned to Stop Worrying and Love the Bomb** 1964

I can't call off the war now. I've paid a month's rent on the battlefield.

Groucho Marx
**Duck Soup** 1933

— Shall we drink to a blitzkrieg?
— I prefer a slow encirclement.

Stanley Ridges and Carole Lombard
**To Be Or Not To Be** 1942

Remember, men, we're fighting for this woman's honor, which is probably more than she ever did.

Groucho Marx
**Duck Soup** 1933

No bastard ever won a war by dying for his country. He won it by making the other poor dumb bastard die for his country.

> George C. Scott
> **Patton** 1970

— Kill every officer in sight.
— Ours or theirs?

> Lee Marvin and Charles Bronson
> **The Dirty Dozen** 1967

— Don't you realize we're facing disastrous defeat? What are you going to do about it?
— I've done it already. I've changed to the other side.

> Groucho Marx and Chico Marx
> **Duck Soup** 1933

— He's certainly Navy.
— So was Captain Bligh.

> Naval Officer and Fred MacMurray about Humphrey Bogart
> **The Caine Mutiny** 1954

The navy is my whole life. Before I was in the navy I was just John Paul Steckler – the meatball. Now I'm Lieutenant John Paul Steckler – the meatball.

Jerry Lewis
**Don't Give Up the Ship** 1959

– Just between us, Schlammer, what did you do during the war?
– I was with the underground.
– Resistance fighter?
– No, motor-mechanic on the subway.

James Cagney and Red Buttons
**One, Two, Three** 1961

– He won a Bronze Star and a Purple Heart.
– Try buying a cup of coffee with them.

Charles Cane and John Payne
**Kansas City Confidential** 1952

# POLITICS

— What do you do for a living?
— I'm a politician.
— I don't like work either.

Mae West and William B. Davidson<br>
**I'm No Angel** 1933

There's always politics. Think what it means
to be a senator. Your mail goes free.

Janet Leigh<br>
**Living It Up** 1954

Politics? Ha! You couldn't get into politics.
You couldn't get in anywhere. You couldn't
even get in the men's room at the Astor.

Jean Harlow to Wallace Beery<br>
**Dinner at Eight** 1933

Politics is a very peculiar thing. If they want
you, they want you. They don't need reasons
any more. They find their own reasons. It's
just like when a girl wants a man.

Harry Hayden
**Hail the Conquering Hero** 1944

I apologize for the intelligence of my
remarks, Sir Thomas. I had forgotten that
you were a Member of Parliament.

George Sanders
**The Picture of Dorian Gray** 1945

— A zombie has no will of his own. You see
them sometimes walking around blindly,
with dead eyes, following orders, not
knowing what they do, not caring.
— You mean like Democrats?

Richard Carlson and Bob Hope
**The Ghost Breakers** 1940

– Do you believe in reincarnation, you know,
that dead people come back?
– You mean like Republicans?

Nydia Westman and Bob Hope<br>
**The Cat and the Canary**  1939

My job is to teach these natives the meaning
of democracy, and they're going to learn
democracy if I have to shoot every one of
them.

Paul Ford<br>
**The Teahouse of the August Moon**  1956

# ROYALTY

– Take this to the Privy Councillor.
– Where is he, Your Excellency?
– Where would a Privy Councillor be? If he's
not there, he'll be with my daughter.

W.C. Fields and Andy Clyde<br>
**Million Dollar Legs**  1932

— Why, you speak treason.
— Fluently.

Olivia de Havilland and Errol Flynn
**The Adventures of Robin Hood** 1932

Problems were never solved by bowing from
a balcony.

Greta Garbo
**Ninotchka** 1939

You don't think I enjoyed what we did this
evening, do you? What I did tonight was for
Queen and Country.

Sean Connery to Luciana Paluzzi
**Thunderball** 1965

# HOME AND ABROAD

# HOME

That's what I like. Everything done in
contrasting shades of money.

> Bob Hope about a fancy apartment
> **That Certain Feeling** 1956


This floor used to be wood, but I had it
changed. Valentino said there's nothing like
tile for a tango.

> Gloria Swanson
> **Sunset Boulevard** 1950


The dining room is to be yellow, and a very
gay yellow. Just ask one of your workmen to
get a pound of the A & P's best butter and
match it exactly.

> Myrna Loy to Emory Parnell
> **Mr Blandings Builds His Dream House** 1948

An experienced caterer can make you
ashamed of your house in 15 minutes.

Spencer Tracy
**Father of the Bride** 1950

Two single men living alone should not have
a house cleaner than my mother's.

Walter Matthau to Jack Lemmon
**The Odd Couple** 1968

It's a nice building. You get a better class of
cockroaches.

James Earl Jones
**Claudine** 1974

Nothing but a fire could help that parlor.

Lana Turner
**Rich Man, Poor Girl** 1938

— Wonderful closet space.
— That's the living room.

Desi Arnaz and Lucille Ball
**The Long, Long Trailer** 1954

217

# TRAVEL

— What are you doing? This is a one-way
street.
— I'm only going one way.

Ryan O'Neal and Barbra Streisand
**What's Up, Doc?** 1972

No phone pole ever hit a truck unless it was
in self-defence.

Alan Hale
**They Drive by Night** 1940

— I proved, once and for all, that the limb is
mightier than the thumb.
— Why didn't you take off *all* your clothes?
You could have stopped 40 cars.
— I'll remember that when we need 40 cars.

Claudette Colbert showing Clark Gable how to hitch
a ride
**It Happened One Night** 1934

— Taxi!...Waterloo.
— The station, sir?
— Well, it's a bit late for the battle.

Tom Adams and taxi-driver
**Where the Bullets Fly** 1966

— I came here on my private boat.
— Yeah, a tramp steamer.

Ann Miller and Keenan Wynn
**The Thrill of Brazil** 1946

— Suppose the ship hit an iceberg and sank,
which one would you save?
— Those girls couldn't drown.

Two Male Passengers about Marilyn Monroe and
Jane Russell
**Gentlemen Prefer Blondes** 1953

I never dreamed that any mere physical
experience could be so stimulating.

Katharine Hepburn riding the rapids with Humphrey
Bogart
**The African Queen** 1951

219

Had the silly thing in reverse.

Daffy Duck backing a space rocket into the earth
**Duck Dodgers in the 24½th Century** 1953

# PLACES

— Is this Kansas City, Kansas, or Kansas City, Missouri?
— This is Wu Hu, China.
— Well, what is Wu Hu doing where Kansas City ought to be?
— Maybe you're lost.
— Kansas City is lost. I am here.

W.C. Fields and Franklin Pangborn
**International House** 1933

Klopstokia...A far away country. Chief Exports: goats and nuts. Chief Imports: goats and nuts. Chief Inhabitants: goats and nuts.

W.C. Fields
**Million Dollar Legs** 1932

— What's the chief export of San Marcos?
— Dysentery.

David Ortiz and Woody Allen
**Bananas** 1971


You know, I've never been able to understand
why, when there's so much space in the
world, people should deliberately choose to
live in the Middle West.

Clifton Webb
**The Razor's Edge** 1946


— I know I'll enjoy Oklahoma City.
— But of course. And if it should get dull, you
could always go over to Tulsa for the
weekend.

Irene Dunne and Cary Grant
**The Awful Truth** 1937


If he had a choice between Hell and Arizona,
he'd live in Hell and rent out Arizona.

Douglas Watson
**Ulzana's Raid** 1972

— You were born in St Louis. What part?
— Why, all of me.

John Miljan and Mae West
**Belle of the Nineties** 1934

— Pretty good town you have here.
— You bet. We have a public library and the
largest insane asylum in the State.

Elise Cavanna and W.C. Fields
**The Barber Shop** 1933

— You've lived here all your life?
— *Twice* as long.

Fredric March and Carole Lombard
**Nothing Sacred** 1937

Living here is like waiting for the funeral to
begin. No, it's like waiting in the coffin for
them to take you out.

Bette Davis
**Beyond the Forest** 1949

222

Pardon, please, is this the way to Europe, France?

> Marilyn Monroe boarding a boat
> **Gentlemen Prefer Blondes** 1953

If I have to go to Honolulu alone, he's coming with me.

> Oliver Hardy
> **Sons of the Desert** 1934

Like Webster's Dictionary, we're Morocco bound.

> Bob Hope and Bing Crosby
> **Road to Morocco** 1942

– Where do you suppose we are?
– This must be the place where they empty all the old hourglasses.

> Bing Crosby and Bob Hope
> **Road to Morocco** 1942

— What in heaven's name brought you to
Casablanca?
— My health. I came to Casablanca for the
waters.
— The waters? What waters? We're in the
desert.
— I was misinformed.

Claude Rains and Humphrey Bogart
**Casablanca** 1942

Shall I tell you how I glittered through the
South Seas like a silver scimitar?

Reginald Gardiner
**The Man Who Came to Dinner** 1941

This picture takes place in Paris, in the
wonderful days when a siren was a brunette
and not an alarm...and if a Frenchman
turned out the light it was not on account of
an air raid!

Prologue
**Ninotchka** 1939

One has to be rich as you, Gaston, to be
bored at Monte Carlo.

> Hermione Gingold to Louis Jordan
> **Gigi** 1958

— Most girls would give their eyes for a
chance to see Monte.
— Wouldn't that rather defeat the purpose?

> Florence Bates and Laurence Olivier
> **Rebecca** 1940

Italy is not a country, it's an emotion.

> Juliet Mills
> **Avanti!** 1972

You know what's wrong with New Mexico?
Too much outdoors.

> Kirk Douglas
> **Ace in the Hole** 1951

New York, you got air you can sink your
teeth into.

Tony Randall
**Pillow Talk** 1959

Atlanta? That's Siberia with mint juleps.

James Cagney
**One, Two, Three** 1961

# NATIONALITIES

Not Gods. Englishmen. Which is the next
best thing.

Michael Caine
**The Man Who Would be King** 1975

I saw that English dame. She looked as if she
was smelling a dead fish.

Jean Harlow
**China Seas** 1935

– Oh, she's not English, darling. She's from Pittsburgh.

– She sounded English.

– Well, when you're from Pittsburgh, you have to do something.

Rosalind Russell and Jan Handzlik
**Auntie Mame** 1958

– Jenny's daughter is still going with that actor.

– An actor? Fashions in sin change. In my day, it was Englishmen.

Lucille Watson and Mary Young
**Watch on the Rhine** 1943

– What is your nationality?

– I'm a drunkard.

Conrad Veidt and Humphrey Bogart
**Casablanca** 1942

— American?
— Yes, except for my father's and mother's
sides. They're Irish.

> Tommy Noonan and Marilyn Monroe
> **Gentlemen Prefer Blondes** 1953

— My ancestors came over on the *Mayflower*.
— You're lucky, now they have immigration
laws.

> Almira Sessions and Mae West
> **The Heat's On** 1943

There can only be one winner, folks, but isn't
that the American way?

> Gig Young
> **They Shoot Horses, Don't They?** 1969

There is no such thing as a great American
lady. Great ladies do not occur in a nation
less than two hundred years old.

> Lotte Lenya
> **The Roman Spring of Mrs Stone** 1961

I have never yet met an American to whom
the American way of life was not his own
particular way of life.

Marius Goring
**The Barefoot Contessa**  1954

Can a nation that belches understand a
nation that sings?

Fortunio Bonanova about the Germans and Italians
**Five Graves to Cairo**  1943

Remember the Spanish word for 'No' is 'No'.

Ann-Margaret
**The Pleasure Seekers**  1964

# NATURE

# ANIMALS

One morning I shot an elephant in my pajamas. How he got in my pajamas I don't know. Then we tried to remove the tusks but they were embedded in so firmly that we couldn't budge them. Of course, in Alabama the Tuscaloosa but that's entirely irrelephant.

Groucho Marx
**Animal Crackers** 1930

I think I'll go out and milk the elk.

W.C. Fields
**The Fatal Glass of Beer** 1933

— Shall we to the hounds?
— Sure, I'd love to meet your family.

Roger Smith and Joanna Barnes
**Auntie Mame** 1958

232

— Do you not wish to give up this inhuman
hunt?
— We're not hunting inhumans, we're
huntin' birds.

Sylvester the Cat and Junior
**Birds of a Feather** 1961

We're caught like rats in a trap. Well, at
least we're a boy-rat and a girl-rat...

Bob Hope to Dorothy Lamour
**My Favorite Brunette** 1947

I started to walk down the street when I
heard a voice saying, 'Good evening, Mr
Dowd.' I turned and there was this big white
rabbit leaning against a lamppost. Well, I
thought nothing of that, because when
you've lived in a town as long as I've lived in
this one, you get used to the fact that
everybody knows your name.

James Stewart
**Harvey** 1950

Hello, Acme Pest Control, I've got a pest I want controlled.

> Elmer Fudd about Bugs Bunny
> **Robot Rabbit** 1953

— How many times have I told you not to take the dog out without a muzzle?
— I put a muzzle on, but I couldn't breathe.

> Bud Abbott and Lou Costello
> **Rio Rita** 1942

I'd horsewhip you if I had a horse.

> Groucho Marx
> **Horse Feathers** 1932

— What is the victory of a cat on a hot tin roof?
— Just staying on it, Ah guess.

> Paul Newman and Elizabeth Taylor
> **Cat on a Hot Tin Roof** 1958

# WEATHER

What a gorgeous day! What effulgent
sunshine! It was a day of this sort that the
McGillicuddy brothers murdered their
mother with an ax.

W.C. Fields
**Poppy** 1936

It's gonna be a hot night and the world goes
crazy on a hot night and maybe that's what
a hot night is for.

Burt Lancaster
**The Rainmaker** 1956

You know, when it's hot like this...you know
what I do? I keep my undies in the icebox.

Marilyn Monroe
**The Seven Year Itch** 1955

How I detest the dawn. The grass always looks like it's been left out all night.

Clifton Webb
**The Dark Corner** 1946

— This is a nice pickle we're in. We're to be shot at sunrise.
— I hope it's cloudy tomorrow.

Oliver Hardy and Stan Laurel
**The Flying Deuces** 1939

— You don't understand. Every night, when the moon is full, I turn into a wolf.
— You and fifty million other guys.

Lon Chaney Jr and Lou Costello
**Abbott and Costello Meet Frankenstein** 1948

Once I tried to let a smile be my umbrella. I got awful wet.

Celeste Holm
**Gentleman's Agreement** 1947

It is easy to understand why the most beautiful poems about England in the spring were written by poets living in Italy at the time.

George Sanders
**The Ghost and Mrs Muir** 1947

# SHOW BUSINESS

# SHOW BUSINESS

Ladies and gentlemen...the world's greatest
novelty: the twins, Redwood and Brentwood...
Redwood, he is the smallest giant in the
world whilst his brother, Brentwood, is the
largest midget in the world. They baffle
science.

> W.C. Fields as a circus owner introduces two
> completely normal men of average build
> **You Can't Cheat an Honest Man** 1939

My act is known all over Europe. That's why
I'm taking it to America.

> Bob Hope
> **The Princess and the Pirate** 1944

That script is an insult to a man's
intelligence. Even mine.

> W.C. Fields
> **Never Give a Sucker an Even Break** 1941

The difference between American and
European movie magnates is astonishing:
there is none.

> Humphrey Bogart
> **The Barefoot Contessa** 1964

An associate producer is the only guy in
Hollywood who will associate with the
producer.

> Fred Allen
> **Sally, Irene and Mary** 1938

We want to produce this play to show the
world the true Hitler, the Hitler you loved,
the Hitler you knew, the Hitler with a song
in his heart.

> Zero Mostel
> **The Producers** 1967

I talked to a couple of yes men at Metro.
They said no.

> William Holden
> **Sunset Boulevard** 1950

– You're not going to catch the opening
night?
– No, I'm going tomorrow and catch the
closing.

> Ginger Rogers and Eve Arden
> **Stage Door** 1937

On our last appearance here the house was
so crowded they couldn't applaud
horizontally, they had to applaud vertically.

> W.C. Fields
> **The Old Fashioned Way** 1934

– The show died in Pittsburgh.
– What do they know in Pittsburgh?
– They know what they like.
– If they knew what they liked, they
wouldn't live in Pittsburgh.

> William Demarest and Joel McCrea
> **Sullivan's Travels** 1941

— Is the show closing?
— Like a tired clam.

> Ginger Rogers and Gail Patrick
> **Stage Door** 1952

It was the kind of flop that made even the audience look bad.

> Fred Astaire
> **The Band Wagon** 1953

This is the screwiest picture I was ever in.

> A camel speaking direct to camera
> **Road to Morocco** 1942

I don't use a pen. I write with a goose quill dipped in venom.

> Clifton Webb as a columnist
> **Laura** 1944

# ACTING

— Actors are not animals. They're human beings.
— They are? Have you ever eaten with one?

> Gene Wilder and Zero Mostel
> **The Producers** 1967

— Are you appearing anywhere now?
— Sure, you can catch me every Friday at the State Unemployment Office.

> Jack Weston and Goldie Hawn
> **Cactus Flower** 1969

She hasn't worked in so long, if she does get the job it'll practically amount to a comeback.

> Eve Arden
> **Stage Door** 1937

— Why, certainly you must have heard of
Hamlet?
— Well I meet so many people.

> Katharine Hepburn and Eve Arden
> **Stage Door** 1937

This place is crawling with celebrities. I'm
the only person here I never heard of.

> Shirley Maclaine
> **Sweet Charity** 1969

What he did to Shakespeare, we are doing
now to Poland.

> Sig Ruman as a Nazi about Jack Benny's acting
> **To Be or Not To Be** 1942

— Any callers?
— Only some child actors. I threw them down
the stairs, and it did my heart good to hear
them bounce.

> Bing Crosby and Ned Sparks
> **The Star Maker** 1939

✓ — You're Norma Desmond. Used to be in
silent pictures. Used to be big.
— I *am* big. It's the *pictures* that got small.

> William Holden and Gloria Swanson
> **Sunset Boulevard** 1950

In a star, it's temperament, but in a chorus
girl, it's just bad taste.

> Charles Lane
> **42nd Street** 1933

# DANCE

— Would you like to dance?
— I don't even like to walk.

> Gale Page and James Cagney
> **The Time of Your Life** 1948

I could dance with you till the cows come home. On second thought, I'd rather dance with the cows till you came home.

Groucho Marx
**Duck Soup** 1933

— Did anyone ever tell you you dance like Ginger Rogers?
— Why, no.
— No wonder.

Ole Olsen and Martha Raye
**Hellzapoppin** 1941

She came at me in sections. More curves than a scenic railway.

Fred Astaire about Cyd Charisse
**The Band Wagon** 1953

You don't have to have feet to be a dancer.

Mae West
**I'm No Angel** 1933

247

Dancing is the most fun you can have
without laughing.

Ann Sheridan to George Raft
**They Drive by Night** 1940

## MUSIC

— That voice!
— What voice?
— Listen. What does it sound like?
— Who'd be selling fish at this hour?

Dorothy Lamour and Bob Hope about Bing Crosby
**Road to Utopia** 1945

Signor Ravelli's first selection will be
'Somewhere My Love Lies Sleeping' with a
male chorus.

Groucho Marx
**Animal Crackers** 1930

I've been a juvenile for 18 years and you're not gonna tell *me* how to sing a song.

Clarence Nordstrom to Dick Powell
**Gold Diggers of 1933** 1933

You're willing to pay him a thousand dollars a night just for singing? Why, you can get a phonograph record of Minnie the Moocher for 75 cents. For a buck and a quarter you can get Minnie.

Groucho Marx
**A Night at the Opera** 1935

The soprano's voice sounded like the brakes on the Rome Express.

Vincent Price
**Serenade** 1956

I guess mine is strictly a bathtub voice.

Claudette Colbert
**Midnight** 1939

Nobody handles Handel like you handle
Handel. And your Delius. Delirious!

Edgar Kennedy
**Unfaithfully Yours** 1948

Don't eat onions tomorrow night.

W.C. Fields advice to a bassoon player
**The Big Broadcast of 1938** 1938

When I heard you were alive, I drank a
bottle of champagne and played Chopin's
funeral march in swing time.

Mary Astor to George Brent
**The Great Lie** 1941

Frederic, you must stop that Polonaise jangle!

Merle Oberon to Cornel Wilde as Chopin
**A Song to Remember** 1945

Well, that's it for tonight, folks. This is Sweet
Sue, saying goodnight, reminding all you
daddies out there that every girl in my band
is a virtuoso – and I intend to keep it that
way.

Joan Shawlee
**Some Like It Hot** 1959

# INDEX

265